THE

Luton Harness

(Late C. PAYNE),

35, PARK SQUARE, LUTON.

A TRIAL SOLICITED.

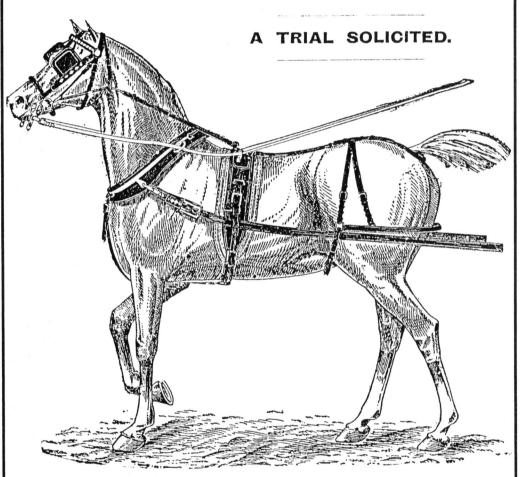

A. T. OLIVER, Proprietor.   B. WHITMORE, Manager.

✳

ALL KINDS OF HARNESS MADE ON THE PREMISES

By Experienced Workmen.

All kinds of WHIPS, BITS, SPURS & BRUSHES. HORSE CLIPPERS by all the Leading Makers. CLIPPING SCISSORS, COMBS, SINGEING LAMPS, HORSE CLOTHING, WATERPROOF APRONS—a Speciality. NEW APRONS FOR SELF BINDERS Made and Repaired.

BELTING OF EVERY DESCRIPTION MADE TO ORDER.

PORTMANTEAUS, DRESS BASKETS AND BAGS REPAIRED.

Special attention given to Lining Cart Saddles and Collars with our specially prepared Collar Checks and New Wool.

LUTON
Scene Again

SCIENTIÆ ET LABORI·DETUR

LUTON
Scene Again

Ken Cooper

Phillimore

1990

Published by
PHILLIMORE & CO. LTD.
Shopwyke Hall, Chichester, Sussex

ISBN 0 85033 775 5

Printed and bound in Great Britain by
BIDDLES LTD.
Guildford, Surrey

This book is dedicated to
The Pudding Stone which started it,
John who encouraged it,
and Mary who kept it on course.

But the past, that alone is ours,
And none can take it from us.
As we may revel in nought else,
Let us revel in that.

Luiz, in W. S. Gilbert's *The Gondoliers*

List of Illustrations

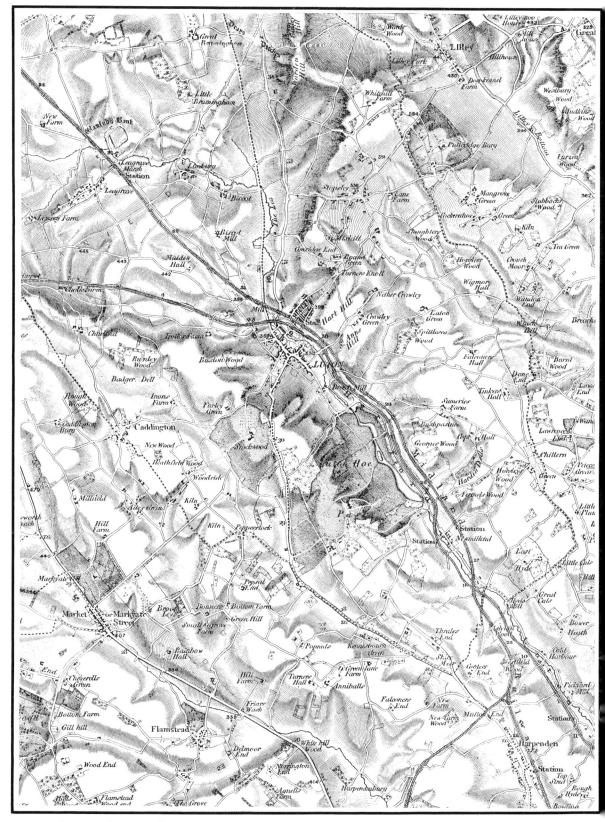

Luton and surrounding area from the first Ordnance Survey map, originally published in 1834.

Luton – Scene Again

Introduction

Several authors have written large, comprehensive histories of Luton, illustrated with photographs which have become well known, perhaps even over exposed. My aim is not to produce another heavy, academic tome. In assembling this book I have tried to highlight a few of the town's salient historical features, illustrated by a collection of less well known photographs. These recall a time which many older Lutonians will probably look back on with feelings of nostalgia. Much changed during the period covered by this book, the end of the 19th century up to the mid-1930s: a rapidly expanding population, road and house building, the Great War, technological advances including improvements in transport, and higher standards of living.

However, this book is not intended for older Lutonians alone. Younger residents will be fascinated to learn how Luton has changed from a small town rooted in the countryside, with a single staple industry of millinery, to become a large industrial centre geared to engineering and a new staple industry in the shape of the motor car.

The Markets of Luton

Luton's markets are almost as old as the town itself and were certainly flourishing at the time of the Norman Conquest. Until the mid-19th century it was common practice to buy and sell livestock in the town centre, principally in the Park Square area, although there were occasional sales of pigs and sheep in Hog Lane and Sheep Street, later renamed Chapel Street and Park Street respectively. In the later years of the 19th century, Monday, which was market day, also saw open stalls selling fruit, vegetables and general goods clustered on Market Hill, Park Square and spilling over into Park Street, a traditional venue for fairs, too. Crowds would come into town from the surrounding villages and hamlets, bringing their produce for sale and buying household goods needed for the following week.

On Mondays all public houses and hotels had extended licensing hours and cashed in on the trade which the market attracted. The hat industry was booming at this time and horse-drawn vehicles taking cartons of hats to the railway yards were inconvenienced by the stalls and animals cluttering the streets. Another disadvantage of this open-air market was the complete absence of public toilets and the inadequacy of those in the public houses and hotels.

Livestock was generally sold by lot at auction, the Council charging a levy on all street sales. Hoping to avoid paying these levies, John Cumberland, a local auctioneer, valuer and general dealer, opened a cattle market on his own property in Castle Street. Fearful of loss of income, the Town Council took him to Court and the justices ruled that even though the market was held on private land this did not exempt him from paying the levy. Despite an appeal, Cumberland had to pay, and eventually reached an agreement with the Council, paying a fixed annual sum. The provision of space in his stockyard took much of the trade from Park Square but the problems of traffic congestion and hygiene remained.

In 1899 the site of the Anchor Brewery in Bridge Street came up for sale and was bought by the enterprising Cumberland. There he established Luton's first purpose-built cattle market. Monday remained market day and the streets in Park Town enjoyed considerable relief. To help matters further, the Council provided public toilets on main street sites and generally improved the town's sanitary arrangements. The Bridge Street market had extensive pens to hold stock awaiting sale, a general yard for the sale of miscellaneous goods, and a separate building to hold poultry, rabbits and game. There was no auctioneer's ring as such, the selling being done on a pen-to-pen basis.

The cattle market continued at the Bridge Street premises throughout the Great War, but in the post-war years Luton gradually expanded and was transformed from a small country town to an industrial community. Once again the streets were jammed with traffic, this time motor-cycles, cars, buses and commercial delivery vehicles. By the mid-1930s it was impractical to continue driving livestock through a town already gearing itself up to face a Second World War. Once again the firm of J. Cumberland and Son provided the answer and the market was moved to new yards between Park Street and Langley Street in 1937. The Park Street facilities were better than those in Bridge Street, but nothing could prevent the decline of Luton as an agricultural centre. The market limped through the Second World War but finally came to an end in the 1950s.

Even after the removal of livestock and poultry from the streets at the turn of the century, trading continued from street stalls for the benefit of townsfolk who bought general provisions on their way home from work. The stalls were lighted with storm lanterns and naptha flares, to augment the dim street gas lamps. Stalls often remained open until 10 o'clock at night, stall-holders shouting out the price of their wares. Travelling salesmen, vendors of herbal remedies, patent medicines and household gimmicks, second-hand dealers and men promising 'painless' tooth extraction and other dental treatments traded alongside the 'permanent and established' regular stall-holders.

By 1924 the Plait Halls had fallen into disuse and were modified for use as a covered market. Alterations to the old buildings were completed in 1925, stalls transferred from the street and an official opening named the complex 'The Market Halls', though most locals referred to it as the Indoor Market or the Covered Market. Many of the street traders had no desire to conform to the rigidity of the fixed pitches in the new market and refused to take up new sites. As a result, much of the atmosphere and colour of the open market was lost on transfer.

The new market soon began to thrive and became popular with housewives wishing to shop cheaply and in the dry. There were three entrances to the Halls, from Market Hill, Cheapside and Waller Street, opposite the Grand Theatre. The amenities for the traders in the permanent building were considerably better than the exposed streets, with toilet facilities, piped hot water, central heating and even a cattery where cats were bred to keep down the rats and mice inevitably attracted to the market.

Many traditions grew up around market life. Older shoppers will remember the ringing of the closing bell by the superintendent – it was last heard in May 1972, before the building was demolished.

Brewing in Luton

Before the hat industry became prominent in Luton, the manufacture of beers and mineral waters provided considerable employment in the town. All the ingredients for brewing beer were available locally: oats (used by J. W. Green for his oatmeal stout) and barley were grown in the surrounding fields and the best quality water required for a fine brew was to be found in the wells sunk into the water-bearing chalk of the Chilterns. Many of the town's breweries were built near the River Lea, which reduced the depth of bore-hole needed and therefore the cost of the bore. Some of the later wells were very deep; for example, the new well at Burr's Brewery, dug in 1828, was 465 ft. deep.

The first stage in the production of beer is to change the barley into malt and this was done in buildings called maltings. Most breweries had their own and it was not uncommon for large houses to have them, too; the Old Vicarage had one, for instance. Here, the barley was spread out on large trays, allowed to sprout and was then dried to make malt. The malt was taken to the brewery, added to sugar, water and yeast and allowed to ferment. Hops were then added to give the beer its traditional bitter flavour.

Although brewing has taken place in Luton for hundreds of years, the great names of local brewers did not appear on the scene until the mid-19th century. On the east side of Park Street, adjoining St Ann's Lane, stood the Burr family's home and brewery. The Burrs had run this brewery for several generations and were so highly thought of in the town that Burr Street, Charles Street and Frederick Street were all named after various members of the family. In 1857 Thomas Sworder, a local solicitor who lived at the Bury House, bought the old Park Street brewery, quickly built a new one in Bridge Street and used the original premises as maltings.

While Sworder was building his new Anchor Brewery in Bridge Street, another plant was being erected in Park Street West. It was called the Phoenix Brewery and was owned by Messrs. H. and F. Pearman. They ran it for 12 years until it was purchased by Mr. J. W. Green. From this time onwards, rivalry between Sworder and Green was extremely fierce. Feuding between the two brewers continued until 1897 when Green bought the Bridge Street premises for £139,000. Smaller breweries were acquired at the same time and they, along with the Bridge Street Brewery, were demolished. All brewing activities were then concentrated at the Phoenix Works, which was renamed the Luton Brewery. The site of the Anchor Brewery was sold to provide a new cattle market and the site of the Old Brewery in Park Street was eventually used as a bleaching and dye works. In 1904 a new maltings was built by J. W. Green in Langley Street. Flowers Breweries eventually took over all Luton brewing enterprises in the 1950s.

Most of the old pubs were 'tied' to one or other of the local breweries. The names of Luton's public houses reflect the town's rural origins: in the 1931 list of licensed premises, 28 of the 109 properties listed have names associated with local crafts or agriculture, for example the *Plough*, the *Harrow* and the *Blacksmiths Arms*.

Luton and the Hat Trade

Many legends have grown up around the origins of plaiting and hatting in the Luton area; in fact, no one can be certain why these twin industries began and settled in Bedfordshire and Hertfordshire. It is certain, however, that by the mid-1700s straw plaiting was being carried out in the cottages of Luton, Dunstable and surrounding villages. Plait produced at this time was very coarse, usually made from the complete pipe of straw. Not until the invention of the splitter, a tool which cut the straw into narrow slivers of equal width, could fine grade plait be made. Responsibility for the invention of the splitter has been claimed by many people, from local plaiters to French prisoners-of-war captured in the Napoleonic campaigns from 1799 to 1815. Many of the prisoners, kept in camps in East Anglia, were certainly adept at fine plait-making and Luton dealers visited them to buy their product because of its quality and low cost.

After the conclusion of the Napoleonic Wars, tariffs were raised on goods imported from France, especially clothes and hats, and also on the straw imported from Leghorn in Italy. As a result there was a ready market for local plait and millinery, now in great demand in London and provincial centres of fashion. This was a time when most middle- and upper-class women owned several hats, each for specific occasions, for example, one for church, one for visiting, one for weddings and one for mourning.

In 1826 a factory was established in George Street for the production of hats and bonnets. This proved to be the beginning of the end for the cottage workrooms. The number of hat factories in the centre of town grew steadily, employing female labour to trim and insert the hat linings. Men were usually employed only for moving and stacking the crates and cartons of finished hats and for blocking or forming the hat shapes from the stitched plait hoods.

Until 1870 plaiting remained the cottage industry it had been one hundred years earlier. The plaiters who lived in Luton would go to the Monday plait market, held in George Street, displaying their wares on open stalls. Villagers who had no means of transport would sell to travelling dealers who would take the bundles of plait to hat manufacturers in Luton, making a profit for themselves in the process. It was not only women who had to work long hours plaiting for a pittance; children, too, were expected to work their fingers raw to supplement the meagre family income. Many children were forced to attend the plaiting schools, where education was minimal and output of plait of paramount importance. Thankfully, these schools closed after the introduction of the 1870 Education Act. This, however, caused shortages in the supply of local plait, but it was more than compensated for by the flood of imported plait from Italy, Switzerland, China and Japan. The cheap plait from overseas caused anger and resentment among the local plaiters. Ugly scenes ensued on Market Hill, leading to the burning of an effigy of a Chinaman made from 'the best quality Chinese plait'!

In 1869 the Plait Halls in Waller Street and Cheapside were opened. They were originally intended to remove the brash and noisy plait market from its traditional site in George Street, much as the cattle market was transferred to an off-street site. It was hoped that plait trading could now take place in a business-like atmosphere, but, with the decline in locally made plait, they were almost redundant as soon as they were opened. Importers of foreign plait used them at first, but gradually their commercial use declined and they became instead public halls where meetings, civic dinners, magic lantern shows and other entertainments were held. Later the Plait Halls became the home of the covered market.

With increasing quantities of high quality plait available, it was fortuitous for the hat trade that a machine capable of sewing plait into hat shapes came into use in 1878. The invention of this sewing machine by Edmund Wiseman speeded up production enormously and Luton's hat trade entered a period of boom. This was the time of large factories and prosperous owners. The factories were clustered in the centre of town and near the railway yards, for orders from all over the world were supplied as well as the local hat dealers.

Naturally the hat trade fostered many associated businesses, all of which contributed to the prosperity of Luton's economy. The bleaching and dyeing trades, gelatine manufacturers, block makers, lining and wicker makers, ribbon weavers and numerous small engineering companies which supplied hat factory machinery all shared in the good times.

Just as the straw hat industry was peaking at the turn of the century new materials appeared on the scene. Felt, derived from the woollen trade, came into vogue in the 1870s and rapidly became popular with milliners and the public alike. The manufacturers approved, too, because the felt hat was suitable for winter wear and helped them cope with the slack season which was such a problem with straw manufacture.

During the Great War almost all Luton's overseas markets were lost and there was also reduced home demand for boaters. During the depression which followed the war, fashion changed so drastically that the hat trade went into a total decline, many manufacturers leaving the business altogether. By the 1930s hat making was no longer Luton's staple trade; it was soon to be replaced by the manufacture of the motor car.

The Coming of Industry

Towards the end of the 19th century the straw hat trade was reaching its zenith, with factories and warehouses in and around the centre of the town and large numbers of smaller home-based workshops in the older terraced streets. Although the manufacture of straw hats included bleaching, dyeing, lining and trimming, there were also engineering businesses supplying vital services. They produced sewing machines and other specialised equipment as well as attending to their maintenance and upkeep. One such firm was Janes Bros. of High Town Road, who advertised as 'Engineers to the Straw Trade'.

In addition to such hat-associated companies, there were already several large enterprises making their names in other fields. These included Hayward-Tyler, who made pumps, rams and mineral water making machinery (and can also claim to have made motor cars in Luton before Vauxhall Motors), and Brown & Green, iron founders, who are credited with building a medal-winning velocipede or boneshaker, an early form of bicycle. There were also Balmforth & Co., boilermakers, and the Davis Gas Stove Company which started with a small iron foundry in Langley Street and then built another foundry in Dallow Road named after the Diamond Gas Cooker which they had introduced in 1897, Queen Victoria's Diamond Jubilee year.

The larger industrial concerns with which the town has become associated had yet to discover the advantages of bringing their factories and workforce to Luton. Shortly after 1900, a New Industry Committee was formed from members of the Town Council and the Chamber of Commerce with the aim of persuading companies looking to expand to come to Luton. The committee offered a good rail service to London, railway sidings and yards if required, cheap and low-rated land, plenty of housing for employees, and good educational and social facilities for their families. The early years of the 20th century witnessed industrial growth such as even the New Industry Committee could not have foreseen. Vauxhall Motors, Commercial Cars, George Kent and Skefco all built factories in Luton and added to the prosperity of the town. In 1914 industry was put on a war footing, with much of its output geared to military requirements. New factories were also built for the manufacture of munitions and aircraft, while the established industries provided staff cars, lorries and service equipment.

Parks and Recreation Grounds

When the New Industry Committee was trying to induce companies to move to Luton, one of the desirable features they stressed was the number of parks and open spaces available to residents. 'Luton has a recreation ground in every electoral ward', the publicity leaflets said, although they did not point out that in the early 1900s there were only three wards in the Borough! Nonetheless, it must be said that the Council did provide much in the way of open spaces for inhabitants to enjoy, variously known as parks, recreation grounds and commons.

The first public park in Luton was indirectly the result of the railway line being laid across the Moor. This left a plot of undeveloped land south of the tracks between New Bedford Road and Dunstable Road. In 1868 John S. Crawley of Stockwood offered to exchange a 40-acre plot he owned near High Town for the undeveloped plot plus the compensation money the railway company had paid to cross the Moor. The Council agreed to this exchange and the responsibility for the management of the site was passed to a committee of trustees. The area became known as People's Park and included Pope's Meadow and Bell Close. After the Incorporation of the Borough an Act of Parliament was passed, shifting the responsibility from the trustees to the Luton Corporation. John Crawley built several streets of houses on the land he acquired as a result of the transaction, among them Moor Street, Francis Street (named after his eldest son) and, inevitably, Crawley Road.

In the early 1900s the Borough established two recreation grounds, one in Dallow Road and the other in Manor Road. The latter was the children's favourite because an accessible stretch of the River Lea passed through it. A further recreation ground was planned for a site in Dunstable Road but, although children played there, it was not officially recognised and opened by the Mayor, Councillor J. T. Harrison, until May 1935.

Probably the best loved pleasure ground in Luton is the formal estate known as Wardown Park. Originally named Bramingham Shott (sometimes Shot), the house was built in 1877 as a family home for Frank C. Scargill, a solicitor who held several local offices – he was at various times Clerk to the Justices of the Peace, Clerk to the Petty Sessions, Town Clerk and Steward of the Manor of Luton. When Mr. Scargill's career took him away from the town, he rented out the estate to Mr. B. J. Forder, whose previous house had been called Wardown; he changed Bramingham Shott to Wardown, too.

In 1903 the Wardown estate was put up for sale for £17,000 but some councillors were reluctant to spend such a large sum of money. However, when interest was shown by prospective purchasers from outside Luton, two councillors, Messrs. Oakley and Hucklesby, purchased the estate themselves for £16,250 and then sold it to the Council for the same price, without making any profit themselves, an act greatly appreciated by the townsfolk. The park was opened to the public in July 1905, followed by a formal ceremony in May 1906.

During the Great War, Wardown House was used as a convalescent hospital for wounded servicemen. Recently, a folded service cap, a relic of those times, was found in the roof while repairs were being carried out. After the war, although many sporting and social events were held in the grounds, the Council took little account of the potential of the striking-looking house, merely using it as tea and refreshment rooms and a temporary home for the Park Superintendent on the first floor. It was not until July 1931 that the Library and Bagshawe collection of historical objects were installed in Wardown House and the building was used as a permanent museum.

In 1921 the town acquired a further recreation ground in the form of a gift from Joan Crawley, daughter of Francis Crawley of Stockwood – on the occasion of her 21st birthday she gave the people of Luton 18½ acres of land on the Dallow Road hills, known as the Downs.

The following year Lady Ludlow (until her marriage to Lord Ludlow in 1919 she had been Lady Wernher, wife of Sir Julius Wernher, Bart., of Luton Hoo) presented the Luton

Hoo Memorial Park to the town in commemoration of her son, Alex Pigott Wernher, who was killed in France during the Great War.

The Era of the Tram

Compared with other major towns and cities in Britain, Luton was slow to accept the need for a tramway system. When the Luton Electricity Undertaking was opened in 1901, however, it acted as a spur. The Town Council, realising that the power to run electric trams was available, sought the sanction of Parliament to instal a system in Luton. A bill was drawn up, submitted to Parliament and the Luton Tramways Act was passed in 1905.

While the bill was being steered through Parliament, the Town Council had appointed a committee to manage the project and select the contractors who would supply the tramcars and create the required infrastructure. It was known as the Electricity and Transport Committee. This was a time of stormy meetings with arguments over the style of vehicles and the routes they would run. Luton's streets were very narrow and the routes selected to service the London Road and High Town lines had sharp bends and curves to be negotiated. Businesses in the main streets were anxious to retain their ability to load and unload goods outside their premises. They feared this would become impossible, especially where passing loops were to be installed. While discussions about routes continued, the committee authorised the general contractor to place letters of intent for 12 cars, to be produced by the United Electric Car Company of Preston, along with the necessary permanent way, overhead cabling and supporting standards, all for the sum of £64,000. The orders were placed early in 1907, with crated deliveries due to start later in the summer. The tram depot, a large brick building in Park Street, opposite Bailey Street, was built and equipped with pits and maintenance facilities. It was here that the crates were delivered and the trams assembled and finally finished in their livery of green and cream.

In October 1907 a start was made on laying the permanent way through the streets and this continued until its completion early in February 1908. Although the technical aspects of the tram system were running according to plan, the administration left a great deal to be desired. For instance, the committee left it too late to book their first choice to officially open the system – David Lloyd George was otherwise committed on the appointed day – and, failing to find a celebrity, the task fell to Mr. T. Gair-Aston, Luton's Liberal M.P.

The tracks were laid and the opening day was rapidly approaching with the system as yet untried. Trials were surreptitiously carried out at dead of night and a single car with interior lights extinguished was run over some of the routes. The following morning Luton was full of talk of the strange rumblings and flashes in the sky, which many of the people living along the route mistook for thunder and lightning. After the successful night trials, there was a route-proving run on 18 February, after which the Board of Trade inspectors gave their seal of approval. This was only three days before the Municipal Opening on 21 February 1908 when three trams, decorated with bunting and flags, left the depot yard and then ran the length of the routes, eventually arriving outside the Town Hall, where the civic dignitaries on board enjoyed a sumptuous lunch. The leading car was driven part of the way by Luton's M.P.; later the Mayor, Mr. H. Arnold, took his place at the controls.

At first everyone wanted to try this new and cheap form of transport. Trams were designed to carry 54 passengers but, in the early days, inspectors sometimes found as many as 150 on board! The new vehicles did have disadvantages, however. They had a short wheelbase compared to the length of the body, so instead of rolling from side to side like a modern bus, they rocked from end to end like a boat. People became quite queasy after short journeys and were often seasick on the ride from Wardown to the terminus in London Road.

Trams had a crew of two, a conductor who collected the fares and a driver who had two driving positions, fore and aft, since the vehicles could be driven in either direction. The first 12 trams were all like this, but the next to be purchased was a single-decker with only one crewman who drove and collected the fares also. This tram spent most of its time on the Wardown route because the population was less dense in that part of town. The single-decker, known as Old Number 13, had the advantage of having an enclosed saloon, giving maximum protection against rain. The upper decks of the original 12 trams were open to the elements. This problem contributed to the demise of the trams in Luton. In the 1920s private bus companies began to compete with the trams, offering comfort, speed and weather-proofing; it was little wonder that the trams lost customers. In 1930, in an attempt to fill their seats, four of the trams were fitted with roofs and windows on the upper decks at a cost of £250 each. The 'passengers carried' figures did improve – in 1930-31 almost 3,500,000 passengers were carried on Luton's trams.

Sadly, though, the scales were heavily weighted against the trams. They were found to be causing unacceptable congestion in the main streets which were now being used by increasing numbers of motor cars, the tracks had become hazardous to cyclists and motorcyclists, and extensive capital expenditure was needed to replace worn overhead cables and support standards. In 1931-32, the last year the trams were operated, their profit was only £29 11s. 8d! After much political wrangling, the tramway system was scrapped and replaced with a municipally owned and run bus service. 'The tramcars on the London Road, Wardown and Dunstable Road routes were discontinued on 29th February 1932 and the Round Green route discontinued on 16th April', according to the minutes of the Electricity and Transport Committee. The new fleet of buses began to run on 1 March 1932. Shortly afterwards the tram tracks were removed from the centre of the town – the end of the tram era in Luton.

Luton's Peace Day Celebrations, 1919

The prospect of a day of rejoicing to mark the successful conclusion of the Great War was not welcomed by everyone in Luton. Some objected to the thought of councillors enjoying a banquet at the ratepayers' expense. Another cause of contention was that the cost of tickets for a proposed ball would be prohibitive and, in any case, only men could buy them which created a furore among townswomen, a boycott and the eventual cancellation of the event. The Council incurred further unpopularity when the commemorative medals ordered for local school children arrived too late for presentation. More serious still, the Council refused to allow demobilised ex-servicemen to hold a drumhead memorial service in Wardown Park. A minor adjustment of the by-laws governing the administration of the Park to allow the service to be held would have altered the course of Luton's history.

On Saturday 19 July 1919 a large crowd assembled in Luton Hoo Park, ready to march through the town to Wardown, passing the Town Hall en route. The theme float was entitled 'Peace Enthroned' and was followed by other decorated vehicles representing business and leisure activities in the locality. The whole procession would be helped on its way by several military bands and contingents of soldiers from local camps. Just as the parade was about to march off, a tableau representing Jack Cornwell, the boy sailor who was awarded the Victoria Cross at the Battle of Jutland, manned by ex-servicemen and naval ratings on leave, asked permission to be included in the procession. The organisers placed them at the rear of the parade but the townsfolk gave them the loudest cheer of all as they passed by.

As the float 'Peace Enthroned' passed through Park Square, one of its wheels got stuck in the tram lines and the spectators good-naturedly lifted it clear to enable it to proceed on its way. This proved to be one of the few light-hearted moments of the day.

As the column approached the Town Hall, through a crowded George Street, Mayor Henry Impey called it to a halt and read a proclamation from King George V which was received in silence by the crowd. The procession moved on but soon came to rest again, whereupon the Mayor repeated the King's words and added some of his own. This was too much for the ex-servicemen, who had arranged to stand near to the civic party at the Town Hall steps. They showered a variety of missiles on the Corporation, who rapidly retreated to the sanctuary of the building, locking the doors behind them. Within seconds the windows of the Town Hall were broken from within and out into the street came the town plate, cutlery and food from the tables set up for the councillors' luncheon. A few ex-servicemen had managed to get into the building along with the retreating Corporation. The Mayor and his party locked themselves in the Mayor's Parlour and there was pandemonium outside in George Street, the crowd shouting 'lynch the Mayor'. Suddenly someone had the presence of mind to ask the band to play the National Anthem. Since many in the crowd had just left the forces they automatically sprang to attention and, for the time being, the trouble subsided. The procession moved off again towards Wardown Park, leaving the crowd to disperse slowly in the rain. Some returned to their homes, but others, including the ex-servicemen's groups, went into public houses. The one most favoured by the rioters was the *Rabbit* in Old Bedford Road, whose landlord was an ex-naval man and sympathetic to the ex-servicemen's cause. In fact, it was he who had organised the Jack Cornwall float in the procession.

The events planned for the rest of the day were not particularly successful – the fun fair, band concert and children's sports all suffered because of the rain. Throughout the town the sole topic of conversation was the disturbances during the procession and what would happen to the Mayor who was still shut in his Parlour.

As the evening drew on, George Street filled with people anxious to witness further developments. They did not have long to wait. As they were joined by spectators from the firework display which had been held on Pope's Meadow, the Town Hall had already been attacked and set on fire with petrol from a nearby garage. As the fire spread through the building, the police smuggled Henry Impey out through a back entrance, dressed as a special constable. The fire brigade was powerless to prevent the conflagration spreading because its equipment, including hoses and couplings, had been destroyed and 14 firemen injured by the rioters. The crowds in George Street cheered as flames and smoke poured from the stricken building. Windows of surrounding properties were broken by the mob and several shops were looted. At Farmer's, a music shop in Upper George Street (see plate 175), grand pianos were dragged out of display windows and rioters started playing the familiar wartime songs including 'Tipperary', 'Pack up your Troubles' and 'There's a long, long trail a'winding'. The crowd joined in with a will, the rendition of 'Keep the Home Fires Burning' receiving the loudest acclaim of all.

It was still raining and the flags hung limply in the main street when the Town Hall clock started striking midnight. The crowd stilled as the chimes rang out. As the last note died away the clock and bell tower collapsed into the building, causing a great column of flames and sparks to soar upwards. The glow in the sky was visible for miles. The troops arrived at this point with fixed bayonets; aided by repeated baton charges by the police in Upper George Street, they quickly quelled the riot.

The following day Luton counted the cost – the Town Hall had been completely gutted and most of the town's records destroyed. The event made headline news not only nationally but even internationally. The Mayor and his wife left Luton and went to live in Sutton-on-Sea, Lincolnshire. During the incident 39 people were arrested and brought to trial later. As an attempt at appeasement, Lady Wernher allowed a drumhead service to be held in the grounds of Luton Hoo Park the following weekend.

Although there were no further incidents, it took several years for the town to settle down again, for without the Town Hall the administration of Luton was dispersed into vacant offices throughout the town centre, while meetings of the full Council were held in the Carnegie Library. It was not until 17 years later, in October 1936, that Luton replaced its old Town Hall with a new one, built on the same site and constructed of fireproof materials.

Shops, Roads and Streets

1. George Street, *c.*1910: a typical scene in a bustling country town. The town hall, the *George Hotel*, a dental surgery and a shoe shop can all be seen, as well as pedestrians busy about their daily tasks.

2. George Street in 1936 presents a very changed scene: a new town hall and war memorial have been constructed, the trams have disappeared, and the *George Hotel* has been modernised and given a new canopy. The building line on the left has been moved back to give a broader aspect.

3. Viewed from the town hall, George Street stretches towards the Corn Exchange and Market Hill. Hat factories still stood in the main street at this time, c.1915, while carts, piled high with packed hats bound for the railway yard, choked the roads to the station. Trams also added to the congestion. The large house on the left was the home of Dr. Horace Sworder, Medical Superintendent of the Sick and Convalescent Home in High Town.

4. A busy day in George Street, c.1910. Children watch with curiosity and perhaps envy as a motorist drives by; men hump hat boxes; there are delivery boys, shoppers, milk floats and horse-drawn wagons. Running into George Street on the right was Adelaide Terrace, a sleazy court where 'nice people' would not venture.

5.   Market Hill, *c.*1920. When this photograph was taken it was market day (Monday) and the traders' stalls with their clutter of rucked tarpaulins, empty fruit boxes, squashed oranges and bruised apples can be seen on the left. On the right, outside the *Plough Inn*, a solid-tyred steam wagon is delivering Salutaris Table Waters.

6.   Most of the buildings shown in this 1915 photograph of Park Square were constructed in about 1880 and demolished to make way for the Arndale Centre. Older Lutonians still speak with affection about Hootons' Penny Bazaar, Milton's the noted jacket shop and Amies the boot and shoe shop. Accommodation for salesmen and shop assistants was often provided in the upper storeys of these large Victorian buildings.

7. Towards the end of the 19th century, Luton's expansion started to knit together what, until then, had been several separate districts into the homogeneous town of today. The names of these communities still exist; fo instance, Park Town, New Town, High Town, Biscot and Bury Park. Most of them had their own church, pubs and shops. The inhabitants were very insular and seldom visited other parts of the town. This view of Park Town in 1910 shows the *White Lion* and many small shops, most of which have disappeared due to wartime bombing, changes in shopping habits, concentrated sales outlets and shopping centres.

8. A policeman and a businessman standing on the Osborne Road Bridge, close to the site of the Brache watermill. To the right of the bridge was an ancient right-of-way called Marslets Path, sometimes spelt Marsletts running along the east bank of the River Lea, past allotment gardens and watercress beds. The path was re-routed along Gipsy Lane when Vauxhall Motors developed the area as a Sports and Recreation Club in 1948.

9. This painting by Alex Austen of the bridge in Park Road must have given many people the impression that this was the only bridge in the town. It was one in a series called 'Beautiful Bedfordshire' which he produced in 1903. The artist, wishing to emphasise the beauty of the scene, has thoughtfully painted trees and scrub to obscure the sewage outfall which discharged into the river at this point. Sewage, factory effluent from the bleaching and dyeing trade, and noxious industrial waste which was dumped in the river, became a serious problem from the early 1800s and heavily polluted the lakes at Luton Hoo and Brocket Hall.

10. Picture postcards showing this rustic view of Park Road were on sale locally in 1904. This one shows a cyclist looking over the bridge at the River Lea as it flowed towards the lake in Luton Hoo Park. At the time of the Norman Conquest one of Luton's watermills, a few cottages and a ford across the stream stood here. The tiny hamlet was called Stapleford and at this point the centre of the river marked the boundary between the districts of East and West Hyde.

11. Crescent Rise is one of the few private roads in Luton and was laid out in the latter part of the 19th century. The large rambling detached houses accommodated the big families of local Victorian businessmen. Standing on Hart Hill overlooking Crescent Road and the Lea Valley, these homes covered the sites of Stone Age dwellings and traces of the terraces and lynches they occupied are the predecessors of the footpaths that criss-cross the area. This snowy scene was photographed in 1912.

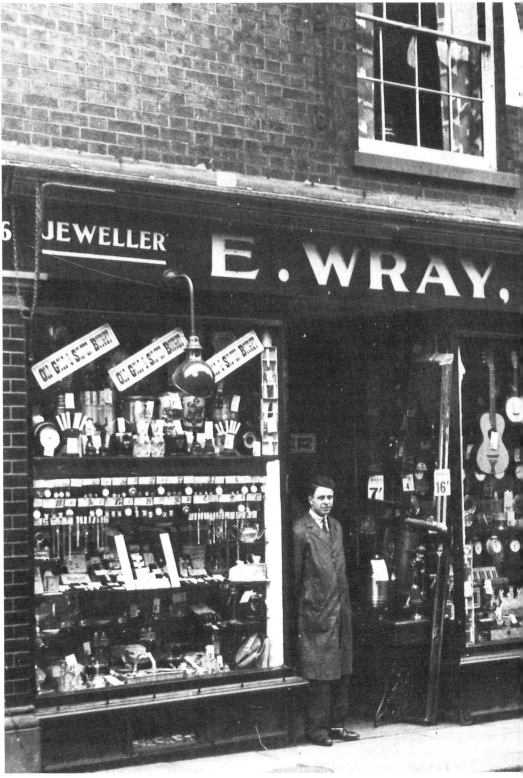

12. Wray's of Castle Street was a family business which started trading in 1913. Jewellery, watches, clocks, ornaments, musical instruments and all kinds of gentlemen's clothing were displayed in the large windows, a diversity typical of the pre-1914 era. Compare Wray's prices with today's. Good quality jackets cost £1.75 or a cheaper one could be had for 35p, trousers ranged from 25p to £1.75, and a new Ingersol pocket watch cost 25p.

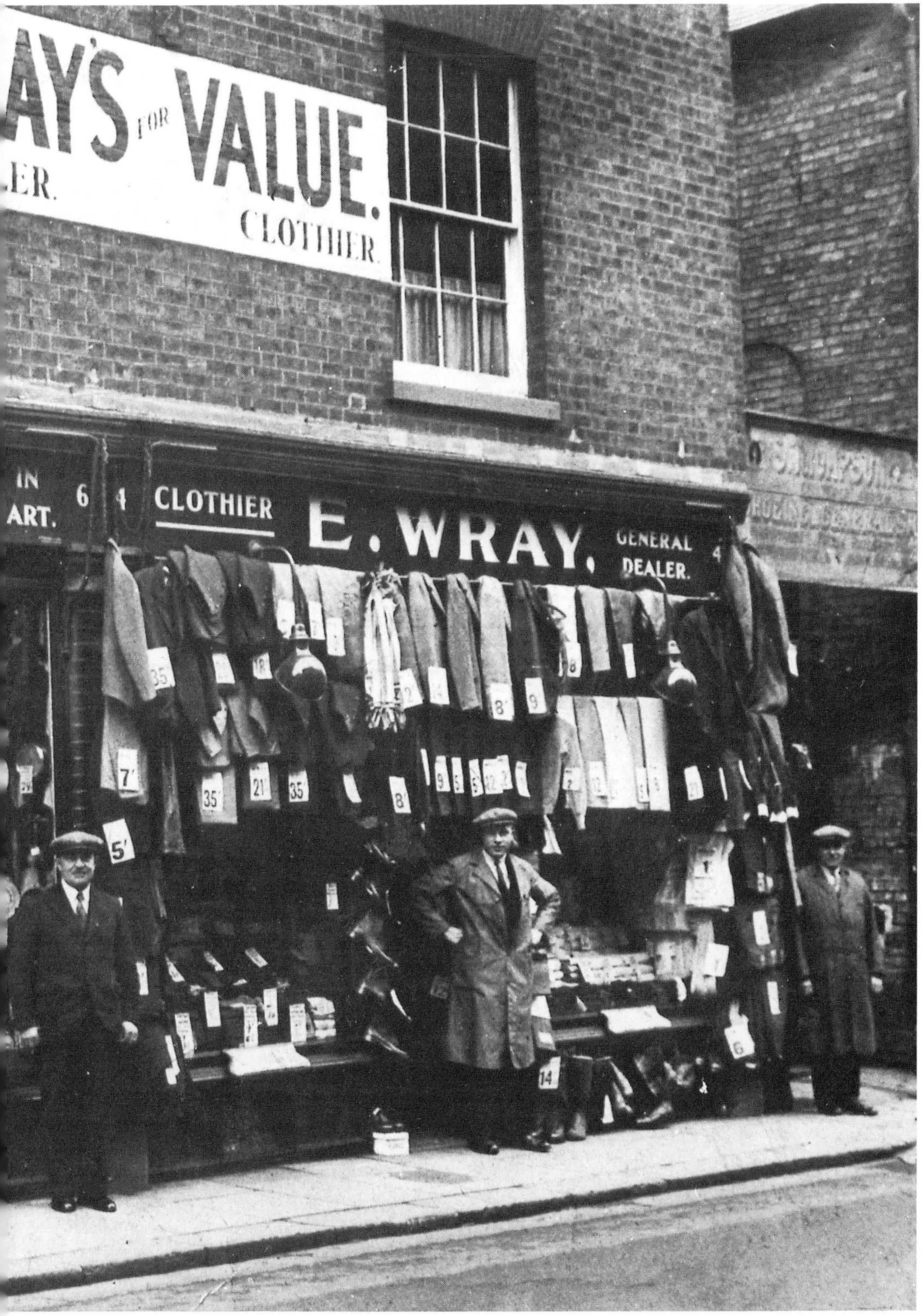
AY'S FOR VALUE.
ER.
CLOTHIER.
IN
ART.
CLOTHIER
E. WRAY.
GENERAL
DEALER.

13.   Castle Parade, seen here around the turn of the century, was situated in Castle Street at its junction with Hibbert Street and Windsor Street. On the left can be seen the Gainsborough Studios of Mr. W. H. Cox, a notable local photographer who specialised in portraits and wedding groups. He also produced many postcards of Luton and its environs; the newsagent's next door displays racks full of them. Castle Parade was demolished in the 1960s and is now a public car park.

14.   A steam-roller, used for resurfacing roads by rolling grit into hot tar, is shown climbing London Road in 1905. The houses on the left stood on the site of Lawn Gardens and Stockwood Court; notice the shoe scrapers by their front doors. The steam-roller bears the brass insignia of a prancing horse with the legend, 'Invicta', the well-known emblem of 'Aveling and Porter', engineers of Rochester.

Luton. Chapel Street.

15.   Chapel Street in the early 1900s. Taking photographs caused quite a stir, stopping paper boys, aproned bakers' boys and staid, bowler-hatted businessmen in their tracks. The London and County Bank, seen on the right, was built in 1897, demolished in 1963 and replaced by the existing building, the National Westminster Bank. Boot's advertising centred more on fine art dealing and Christmas cards than cash chemists at this time!

16.   Horwood's Game, Poultry and Fishmerchant's shop stood in Chapel Street, where it sold pheasants, partridges, turkeys, chickens, hares and a few scrawny rabbits. Below the poultry and game, the wet fish was set out on the spotless white marble slab. Favourites for many would be the piles of shrimps, cockles, whelks and winkles, quickly purchased and taken home for Saturday tea.

17.   An early photograph of J. Cumberland & Sons' cattle yard at the rear of their premises in Castle Street, *c*.1890. John Cumberland, wearing a top hat and waving a gavel, can be seen auctioning a bullock. The buildings and chimney in the background are the remains of the old Phoenix Brewery, purchased by J. W. Green in 1862.

18.   By the end of the 19th century it became obvious that the selling of cattle in the town streets was no longer practical. There were no toilet facilities for traders, at the end of the day the streets were left in a filthy condition and the hat trade traffic passing through the town to the railway was considerably hindered. In 1899 the site of the Anchor Brewery in Bridge Street became available, was purchased by John Cumberland and turned into an off-street cattle market. The traditional Monday market day was retained and traffic congestion in the main streets was considerably relieved.

19. Before the market stalls were moved into the vacant Plait Halls, Luton's general market was held in the open-air around Park Square. Travelling fairs also made use of this area in the town centre. You can see one of the 'rides' on the right. Notice the stall selling rabbits on the left. The shops beyond the fair and trams were built about 1880.

20. This aerial view of the 'old' market in the mid-1930s shows the length of the main Plait Hall, crowded with bargain-hunters.

The Market Cheapside, Luton.

21. Cheapside in 1930. The name is derived from an old Saxon word meaning market, so this old street running between Guildford Street and George Street was aptly named when Luton's covered market was sited there. Originally the building was called the Plait Halls, where straw plait, used in the local hat trade, was bought and sold. The foundation stones for the halls were laid in 1868, by Mr. A. P. Welch, a local plait dealer and philanthropist. The halls had other uses, too; for instance in 1897 Queen Victoria's Diamond Jubilee was celebrated by the old people of the town sitting down to a hearty dinner there. As the straw hat industry declined, the halls fell into disuse and, from 1925, the market that had been held in the streets was housed here under one roof. The site is now under the Arndale Centre.

22. Waller Street took its name from the Waller family who owned property in this part of Luton in the early 19th century. They were prominent hat and bonnet manufacturers and also dealt in straw plait. The street contained several interesting buildings, among them the Public Baths and Winter Assembly Hall, a chapel, the Plait Halls, the Grand Theatre and a Senior Boys' School. The picture shows the street as it was in the early 1900s. The whole street was demolished to make way for the Arndale Centre.

23.   Bute Street was named after a former Lord of the Manor who lived at Luton Hoo. The photograph shows the view looking towards the L.N.E.R. station in about 1908. Hat factories and associated businesses such as ribbons, cottons and veiling lined the street and made it one of the town's most vital thoroughfares.

24.   Whether viewed from top or bottom, photographs of Wellington Street guarantee an interesting glimpse into the past. Many of the buildings in this turn-of-the-century view are recognisable today, although only the *Wellington Arms* serves its original purpose. The street was crowded with a wide variety of businesses, smart dress shops, gents outfitters, house furnishings, fancy goods and a music shop, all combining to make this one of the most popular shopping streets in the town.

25.   Until 1823, the area now covered by Wellington Street was farmland with cows grazing the lush pasture. It was at this time that the Marquis of Bute, Lord of the Manor of Luton, engaged a civil engineer to cut a new road between George Street and Stuart Street. Named after the 'Iron Duke', the road was lined with shops which attracted crowds of shoppers. When this photograph was taken in 1906, Mrs. Baker, Milliner and Ladies Outfitter, occupied the corner shop on the left, while on the right, H. E. Cocker the chemist encouraged people to sample his American-style soda fountain.

26. Messrs. E. Deacon and Sons' Watchmakers, Jewellery and Fancy Goods Emporium at the junction of George Street and Wellington Street always attracted a good number of window shoppers. They came to see the enormous range of merchandise on display, from cabin trunks and fashion clothing to dinner services and barometers. This photograph, taken in 1906, shows women gazing at the wares on offer while the men stand and chat, hoping they won't be asked to part with too much money.

27. John Webdale and Sons Ltd. was opened as a general store in Wellington Street in 1840. The shop traded for over one hundred years and in 1881 John Webdale, its founder, was made Mayor of Luton. Always ahead of its time, Webdale's was constantly expanding and adding to the showrooms to display its stock. It was also one of the first shops in Luton to have a telephone installed.

RAMESES UNDERWEAR

28.   When King Tutankhamun died in 1340 B.C., who could have prophesied that he would be indirectly responsible for this window display in Wellington Street, Luton, in 1924? The Pharaoh lay in his tomb near Luxor for more than 3,200 years until discovered in 1922 by Howard Carter the Egyptologist. The imagination of the public was so stirred by the find that anything associated with Egypt was sure of business success. Rameses, another Pharaoh, soon became a trade name, especially in gentlemen's underwear. Hence the association of Luxor and the Valley of the Kings and Mr. A. Taylor's outfitter's shop at No. 60 Wellington Street.

29. An appreciative audience of men and boys stand and watch the kerbstone laying and pavement repairs taking place outside the public library. In 1913 the slower pace of life enabled them to take time off to stand and stare. This view of George Street and Manchester Street is peopled entirely by men, begging the question, 'Where are all the women?'.

30. Two Luton landmarks which have seen little change since their erection are the railway bridges spanning New Bedford Road. The first bridge carried the Luton, Dunstable and Welwyn Junction Railway when built in 1860 and the second, which was erected eight years later, was for the London, Midland and Scottish Railway. The laying of the latter line led to the demolition of North Mill, one of Luton's Domesday watermills.

31. New Bedford Road, lined with many flowering trees, has always made an impressive entry into Luton from the North. On the Moor, the common land to the west of the river, stood the Pest House. Here, in a small cottage, patients suffering with infectious diseases were treated in isolation. This tiny hospital was built in 1724 and demolished in the late 1800s.

32. One of the two lodges guarding the entrance to Wardown Park in New Bedford Road, 1906. On its acquisition, the Council spent over £6,000 in tree-planting and laying-out the grounds. This sum also included making the ornamental lake, boathouse, bridge, bowling green, tennis courts and a cricket pitch.

33.   It is hard to imagine that the Old Bedford Road, which today borders school playing fields and housing development, was once the main road between Luton and Bedford. Shown on early maps as Barton Road, it lost its importance with the opening of the New Bedford Road in 1832. As can be seen, the old road was not made up in the same way as modern roads and in wet weather quickly became rutted and often impassable.

34.   This view of Old Bedford Road in the vicinity of Wardown Park shows Pope's Meadow on the right, obscured by hedges and trees. Shortly after this photograph was taken in about 1910 the hedge was removed, giving an open vista of the meadow's quiet slopes. On the right, today's landscape is built-up with large family homes overlooking the park. Note the telegraph poles with their gleaming insulators.

35. Lovers Walk runs between the Old and New Bedford Roads, following the boundary of
Wardown Park. It replaced part of an ancient track which in former times connected High
Town with Biscot and Limbury. When the land was acquired in 1875 by Mr. F. C. Scargill,
a solicitor and clerk to the justices, who built himself a house and park called Bramingham
Shott (the old name for Wardown), it took a hearing at the Court of Quarter Sessions in
Bedford to get the old path, which ran through the property, closed and the new path we know
as Lovers Walk substituted in its place.

36. High Town Road *c*.1910: horses and carts, a delivery barrow and Luton Tramways' Car No. 11 make up the traffic in this picture. The tram is on its way to Round Green and shows how unsuitable these electrically-propelled vehicles were in the narrow streets of the town. The cottages adjacent to Harris' Path were demolished in 1911 to make way for the High Town Electric Picture Theatre. Note the barber's pole outside the shaving saloon on the left.

37. The cottages mentioned above have now been demolished and replaced by the High Town Electric Picture Theatre, later renamed the Plaza Cinema. The Picture Theatre is showing a film of General Booth, founder of the Salvation Army, speaking at a rally in London. Talkies had not been invented so presumably his speech was delivered with the aid of sub-titles. Most men enjoyed the luxury of being shaved by a barber – for only 1½d!

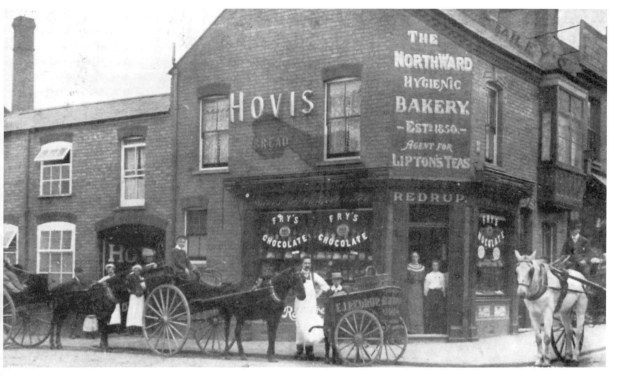

38.   This photograph shows the workforce and vehicles of Fred Redrup's Bakery in 1911, before starting out on the day's deliveries. Mr. F. J. Redrup founded the North Ward Hygienic Bakery in 1850 in premises on the corner of Cross Street and High Town Road and later expanded to become the largest bakery in Luton as Redrup and Starkings. The company owned shops in several parts of the town, each decorated in red and white livery. Prominently displayed in all the shops was a notice which said 'The ideal of this company can be summed up in one word – Service'.

39.   Stuart Street has been totally transformed by the changes made to the town since 1970. Of the houses, shops and pubs shown in this 1916 photograph, only three buildings remain. The rest were demolished to make way for a ring-road on the south-west side of the town. Shaded by the trees on the left is the Court House and Police Station, originally built in 1858 and rebuilt in 1936.

40. This shop, one of 120 tobacconists listed in the 1930 Luton Trade Directory, stood in Stuart Street and displayed in its window an amazing range of tobacco-related products. There were boxed pipes, cigarette holders, cigar piercers, roll-your-own machines and cigarette papers as well as strangely named bowls of tobacco, like shag, plug, sweepings and cut Cavendish. The interiors of these little shops had a smell all of their own, for in addition to the wide variety of tobaccos, many of which were scented, there were several types of aromatic snuff, sold in small tins or loose in transparent envelopes. Another of the tobacconists listed, at 329 Dunstable Road, was appropriately named Mr. P. Uff!

41. Stuart Street, c.1906. The large shop on the left, at the corner of Wellington Street, still exists and, typical of many of the older properties in the area, the window surrounds are made of reconstituted stone, a hard weatherproof substance. The fittings and fixing point for the splendid gas-lamp on the corner are still in situ, although the pipework and shade have long since disappeared. Overshadowing all is the spire of King Street Congregational Church, a landmark for miles around. The church was built in 1865 and demolished in 1970 due to structural faults.

42. When this photograph was taken in 1906, today's ring-road and its complicated junction with Cardiff Road and Inkerman Street were not even thought of. It shows an autumnal view of Council workmen clearing the road with implements reminiscent of large dust-pans attached to broom handles. The gas-lamp which lit this junction had no less than six mantles to boost the illumination.

43.   Dunstable Road has seen sweeping changes over the last 80 years. Once a quiet, peaceful road called Dunstable Lane, it was lined with creeper-festooned houses, each with its neatly-fenced garden. The character of the road altered with the coming of the Corporation Tramways in 1908. The Victorian houses were turned into shops and their gardens became paved forecourts. The trees on the left bordered a flat field where Luton Town Football Club played their home games and which in a later development became the site of the Odeon Cinema.

44.   Dunstable Road in 1902. The horse-drawn cart is approaching the junction with Ivy Road, on the corner of which is a newspaper and tobacconist's shop. Notice the relic of Victorian affluence, a monkey puzzle tree, planted in the garden on the left.

45. In 1906 this general store at the junction of Leagrave and Dunstable Roads was opened to serve the people in Bury Park. It belonged to the Luton Industrial Co-operative Society Ltd. and was the third branch to be established in the town. As in many other parts of Luton, underground springs rise to the surface here in wet weather and it became necessary to fit a pump in the Co-op basement to get rid of the water during winter months. Note the horse trough near the gas-lamp outside the shop.

46. Although there are loaves in the window of No. 273 Dunstable Road, this was not a bakery but a high-class pastry cook and confectioner's business. Shops selling such a varied selection of cakes are few and far between in the Luton of today. However, in 1926 Mr. Stiles' shop offered rock cakes, long iced buns, mince-meat slices, shiny topped currant buns, doughnuts, swiss rolls and jam tarts; while for children the shelves inside the shop were loaded with glass jars filled with tempting sweets of all kinds.

47. Dallow Road Recreation Ground is the smallest of the four 'recs' in Luton, having an area of 5½ acres. It was provided for the people living in the old West Ward division. This view, which also shows part of Ashburnham and Brantwood Roads, has changed remarkably little since the photograph was taken in 1911.

48. The majority of houses in Dale Road were built between 1910 and 1914 to provide rented accommodation for the influx of workers in new industries settling in the Dallow Road and Kingsway areas. The weekly rental of these premises depended on the style and interior fittings used in their construction. At first glance the houses look alike but on examination variations become apparent. Gables and bays were optional extras and the elevations differ on either side of the street, highly decorated on one side and rough cast on the other.

49. Norton Road in Limbury has always had a cold, bleak appearance and this photograph, taken in 1919, is no exception. Both footpaths and road are unmade and show the ruts and puddles caused by the iron-tyred wheels of the tradesmen's carts. Beyond the houses on the right lies Norton Road School, built by Bedfordshire County Council in 1913 to accommodate 384 children.

50. This photograph shows Leagrave Marsh as it was in 1904. The railway and the early buses brought crowds to Leagrave, regarded as the source of the River Lea, earning it the title, 'the blocker's seaside'. A blocker was a hat-worker who formed the shape of hats by pressing felt hoods under heat and steam. The bridge carrying the railway main line can be seen to the right of the houses while the building behind the geese is the *Three Horseshoes*.

Buildings, Chapels and Churches

51.   A Wesleyan Mission was founded in Ashton Street in 1883. This photograph shows the Mission Band in 1898, with the leader of the Mission, Mr. James Gillam, sitting to the left of the woman with the auto-harp. He was so respected locally for his good works that Ashton Street was renamed Gillam Street in his honour. It was from this band that musicians, wishing to play a greater range of music, broke away and formed what was later to become the Luton Band.

52. Before and during the Great War, land on either side of Dunstable Road was developed to provide homes for the growing influx of workers. Until the early 1920s this north-western area of Luton was part of the parish of Christ Church but because of the population expansion it was decided that another church was needed. With money collected from local businesses, a building was erected on land purchased in Shaftesbury Road and called All Saints' Church. After its consecration in 1923 it became the parish church of a new and separate parish.

53. Bailey Hill Wesleyan Church was built in 1898, at the junction of Albert Road and Baker Street. This striking modern church replaced an earlier chapel in Albert Road. Bailey Hill, as it was known locally, was renowned for its flower shows, harvest festivals and Sunday School anniversary services. The church was demolished in the 1960s and replaced with a block of flats.

54. Bailey Hill Church had many outside activities centred on the hut in the church grounds. The Bailey Hill Brotherhood, a church group for men, held its meetings there as did the Women's Fellowship and Sunday School. The Brotherhood also ran a football team which played in the Luton League. The brick structure in the background of this photograph, taken *c.*1918, is the Bailey Hill water tower. The man standing second from the right in the back row was destined to become mayor of Luton, from 1938 to 1944, was granted the Freedom of the Borough in 1945 and knighted to become Sir John Burgoyne, O.B.E., J.P.

55. The village of Biscot had a windmill for over 400 years, the first one being a post mill which stood in Windmill Field. When a new lease was drawn up for the tenancy in 1711, Issac Freeman's name appeared on the document. It was the start of the long association of the Freeman family with milling in Luton; at one time the family also worked the watermill in Mill Street. The tenancy was for 500 years at a rent of sixpence per year. This came to an abrupt end when the mill was struck by lightning in 1841 and burned to the ground. It was rebuilt three years later, much as the photograph shows. The last owner was Mr. Tooley who, in 1926, removed the sails and milled by electric motor. The 'smock' gradually deteriorated and was dismantled in 1938. This photograph was taken in 1920.

56. Biscot Church and Schools were built by
J. Sambrook Crawley of Stockwood, Lord of the
Manor of Biscot, at his own expense in 1867. Until
that time, Biscot was a hamlet with only a handful
of cottages and a windmill. At the time of the
compilation of the Domesday Survey in 1086, the
extent of the hamlet of Biscot was 10 carucates of
land. It is difficult to ascertain the exact area of
these old land measurements, but a carucate was
probably the area of land that could be ploughed by
a team of oxen in a year.

57. The Old Brewery Yard, Park Street, 1900.
Originally the site of Burr's Brewery, the buildings
and yard were purchased by Thomas Sworder in
1857. Having built a new brewery in Bridge Street,
he used the Park Street premises as a maltings.
Other changes in the fortunes of the Old Brewery
Yard saw it used as a small theatre, a dyeworks for
straw plait and a felt hood factory where basic
shapes were made for the hat trade.

58. Bury Park Congregational Church was built in 1903 to serve the residents of the rapidly expanding estate being erected on the fields of Bury Farm. The first houses were occupied in 1882 and the church school halls opened in 1895. The church has seating for congregations of 600 people, the pews being arranged in a semi-circle around the pulpit and in a gallery at the rear.

59. On 5 October 1904 Mr. Joseph Chamberlain, a prominent Conservative, came to Luton to deliver a major political speech on Tariff Reform. It was anticipated that over 6,500 people would come to hear him and, since there was no building in the town large enough for a crowd of that size, a wooden pre-fabricated hall was assembled in Biscot Road. It had dressing rooms for the speakers, flush toilets and was lit by high luminosity gas-lamps. A feature of the hall was the sounding board, hung over the speaker's rostrum; it was designed to eliminate echoes and project the speaker's voice out to the audience. The building survived for two or three years, but by 1908 George Kent's factory was occupying the site.

60. On the afternoon of 1 October 1910 history was made here on the corner of George Street and Williamson Street. The group of town dignitaries is standing on the steps of the new Public Library awaiting the opening by Mr. Whitelaw-Reid, the American Ambassador. He is on the right of Mr. Smith, the Town Clerk. Next to him is the philanthropist Andrew Carnegie, who gave the library to the town, followed by the Mayor Albert Wilkinson. The men in the road are taking a ciné film of the event which was shown at the Anglo-American Electric Picture Palace in Gordon Street the very same evening.

61. Following the opening of the Bute Hospital, a small unit for the nursing of children was established at the Cottage Hospital in High Town Road. Additional space was soon required and, through the effort and financial backing of Mr. A. P. Welch, J.P., the Children's Home was built and equipped in London Road. Although the notice board states 'Founded in 1889', the foundation stone was laid in 1893 by Lady Battersea and the home was opened the following year by the Duchess of Bedford.

62. From its inception, Christ Church was beset by financial and structural problems. Erected on the corner of Dunstable Road and Upper George Street, the foundation stone was laid in 1856 by Mrs. J. Crawley of Stockwood and the first services were held the following year. Unfortunately, the foundations were dug in clay, causing subsidence which necessitated rebuilding. Buttresses were added to the tower and eventually the spire was reduced in height. In 1861 a grand bazaar was held at the Old Brewery in Park Street, to clear debts incurred in the church's construction. Christ Church became the second independent parish of Luton after St Mary's.

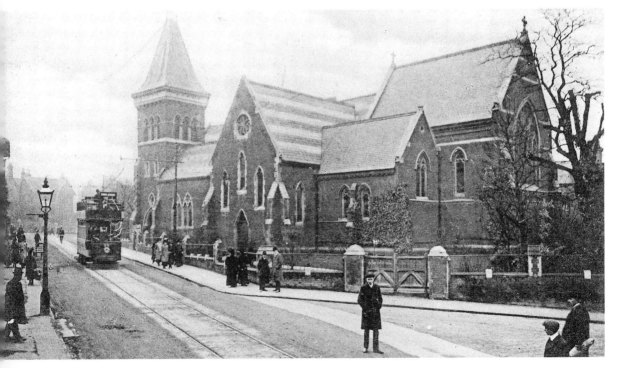

63. In 1886 the Co-operative Wholesale Society opened a factory in London for packing and selling tea. Because of increased demand the company moved to Luton and, in September 1902, built a new factory in Dallow Road. Known as 'The English and Scottish Joint Co-operative Wholesale Societies', production was concentrated on cocoa and chocolate confections. The surrounding district became impregnated with the sickly smell of cocoa when the factory was working and local residents would pray for wind to disperse the appetite-destroying odours.

64. This attractive advertising trade card, showing the collection and shipping of cocoa beans to the Luton factory, was printed and in circulation shortly after the opening of the cocoa works, as it was called locally. As well as producing packaged cocoa, the company marketed an enormous range of confectionery including boxed chocolates, chocolate bars and Easter eggs which sold in Co-op shops all over Britain.

65. The Commercial Cars Co. was founded in London in 1905 and came to Luton the following year, building a factory in Biscot Road. The first year's production in their new home was seven lorries. However, output increased annually and in 1909 Commers unveiled their first double-decker omnibus. During the Great War they were a major supplier of vehicles to the army, but were badly hit financially by the post-war depression and were eventually taken over by Rootes in 1928.

66. The *Coopers Arms* is a small public house situated in Bute Street. Although the ground-floor doors and windows have been modified since the photograph was taken in 1910, the façade is recognisable today. Many pub and inn names in Luton are associated with country crafts, for instance the *Blacksmiths Arms*, *Shepherd and Flock* and *Wheelwrights Arms*. Coopers were the craftsmen who made casks and barrels for storing and transporting brewers' products.

67. The Corn Exchange, purchased by Luton Council for £8,000 from Sir Julius Wernher on 10 July 1911. The Exchange served many purposes in its life apart from corn chandlery – magic lantern and film shows, lectures and political meetings, the manorial and leet courts, concerts, bazaars, dances and exhibitions were all held in this pseudo-gothic building. There are still many people who recall the White Rose Café in the basement. The Corn Exchange was erected in 1869 and demolished in 1951.

68. The interior of the *George Hotel*, one of the most ancient inns in the town, dating back to the 16th century and originally called the *George and Swan*. In 1781 Dr. Samuel Johnson dined here on his way to visit Luton Hoo, as did Messrs. George and Robert Stevenson in 1842, when they met town dignitaries to discuss the building of the railway between London, Luton and Manchester. It even served as the petty sessional court from the 1820s until the building of the town hall in 1846.

GEORGE HOTEL
LUTON
AA*** RAC
TELEPHONES
654 & 613
HOT & COLD SOFTENED WATER
GARAGE 100 CARS

69.   The Ebenezer Chapel stands at the corner of Hastings Street and Dumfries Street. It was built in 1853 at a cost of £950, to accommodate a growing congregation of Particular Calvinistic Baptists. Shortly after completion, a school hall was added to the rear of the chapel, where children from the locality would flock to attend bible classes on Sunday afternoons. At this time morning and evening services were held, with more than 500 worshippers packing the pews to listen to their first and much loved pastor, Arthur Cook.

THE
COUNT of LUXEMBOURG

Grand Theatre,

LUTON.

NOVEMBER 5th,

FOR SIX NIGHTS,

Miss Blanche St. Albans

AND

Mr. J. Leicester Jackson's

PRINCIPAL COMPANY

In the Greatest Domestic Drama of the
present day –

"Her One Great Sin,"

FROM THE

Fulham, Dalston, Stratford, Hammersmith, Islington, New Cross, Standard, and Brixton Theatres, London.

70a. & b. When the Grand Theatre was opened by Miss Lily Langtry in 1898, the first production was 'The Sign of the Cross', a play with a religious message. It was thought at the time to have been chosen to appease the nonconformist community, which was up in arms because there were licensed bars in the theatre. The 'Gaff', as it was known, catered for all tastes of entertainment, from rep to review, magic lantern to films, music hall to pantomime, illusionists to opera, and political meetings to religious services. Touring versions of the great London and American musicals often visited the theatre and the famous names who walked the boards here are legion. The theatre closed in 1957, and was turned into a supermarket and offices. Little did shoppers at Tesco realise that the splendid ceiling and proscenium arch were hidden behind the shop's façade.

71. As trade expanded towards the end of the 19th century, new streets and houses became necessary to cope with the influx of labour hoping to share in the growing prosperity. Builders eager for sales started to name houses as well as number them, to give enhanced social standing to the purchaser and house, too. For example, the deeds of this Victorian villa, standing at the junction of Ashburnham Road and Grove Road, refer to it as Hardwick House, fancifully named after a stately home in Derbyshire.

72. Originally part of the Manor of Lewsey, the Leagrave Hall Estate belonged to the Filmer family. The mansion shown in the photograph was built in 1850 by Sir Edmund Filmer; it is from members of this family that nearby Filmer Road takes its name. In 1868 the Hall was bought by Walter Thomas Lye, a local dyer and businessman, whose improved ribbon weaving techniques and the introduction of aniline dyes gave a greater range of trim and colour to the hat industry.

73. In 1908 the Edward VII School was built in Park Street on the site of 'The White House', home of Thomas Burr the brewer. When the school opened it had accommodation for 300 pupils, half of them being girls. After the Great War ended, the girls were moved to a new school in Alexandra Avenue. The name of the school on Park Square had by then been changed to the Luton Modern School and classes were held there until 1938 when the whole school moved to new premises on Bradger's Hill.

74. The building seen on the right in this 1914 view of New Bedford Road was the premises of E. Ward and Co. Ltd., one of the up-market shops of the town. As well as selling fashionable hats and clothing, there was an adjoining restaurant called the New Bedford Dining Rooms where the smart set enjoyed tea dances and dined in the evening. An outstanding feature of the building was the massive oak staircase which gave access to the dining rooms and dance floor upstairs. On the left is the corner of Alma Street with the butcher's shop which was later demolished to make way for the Alma Cinema.

75. When E. Ward and Co. Ltd. of New Bedford Road closed their shop and tea rooms in 1926, the Luton Industrial Co-operative Society built a new departmental store on the same site. When the Co-op was being erected the lovely oak staircase from Ward's was incorporated within the new building. Although there were other stores in the town, they could not match the 200-ft. long Co-op for size. When this prestigious store, unimaginatively called the Central Premises, opened in March 1927, shoppers crammed into the boot and shoe, outfitting, hardwear and furnishing departments. They could not believe the quantity of stock available or the amount of space to view it.

76.   The Palace Theatre stood in Mill Street and was opened on Boxing Day 1912. Planned as a theatre, it settled down to showing films with variety acts and its own orchestra on stage between performances. Its proscenium arch, decorated with gilt cherubs, was flanked by lavishly appointed boxes, although because of distortion when viewing films they were not often used. A scheme to have shops in the basement and a Wurlitzer cinema organ was abandoned due to water seepage from the River Lea, which ran in a culvert under the building. Successive name changes, including the Gaumont Cinema and Majestic Ballroom, strove in vain to attract customers. As a bingo hall it proved popular, only to be destroyed by fire in December 1982.

77.   The escape from the cares of the world provided by the flickering moving pictures at the local cinema was usually reflected in the decoration of their entrance halls. Once the queue of prospective film-goers had passed the pay kiosk, they found themselves in a completely different world: deep pile carpeting, highly polished brass handrails and door handles, wrought-iron balustrading and dark red drapes. Pride of place went to the electrically-lit chandelier, although there was also auxiliary gas lighting in case of power failure.

78.   The site of the mock-Tudor Post Office, demolished in 1973, is now covered by the Arndale Centre and its location marked by a wall plaque. To the left was an ancient footpath known as Barber's Lane. It took its name from an influential family named Barbar or Barbour who had their home close by. Legend states that the lane was part of the processional route taken by members of the Guild of the Holy Trinity as they paraded the town on holy days. The River Lea crossed the lane near here at a small ford and footbridge which became known as the Guild's Ford. An adjacent road became associated with this old river crossing and gave us today's name, Guildford Street.

79.   The Post Office building in Cheapside was erected in 1881 and used as the General Post Office until the move to new premises in Upper George Street in 1923. The photograph shows early morning roll-call being carried out by the Postmaster, when postmen and telegraph boys were checked for attendance and correctness of uniform prior to collection, sorting or delivery duties.

80. Because of increased postal and telephone business after the Great War, a new General Post Office and Telephone Exchange was built in Upper George Street. The official opening of the new office and the closure of the old one in Cheapside took place in 1923. The new building stood close to the site of Peddar's House, demolished in 1899, one of the last farmhouses in the centre of the town. An interesting sign on the left of this picture reads, 'Warning. Narrow space between trams and kerb'. Positions like this were known as tram pinches.

81. Although incorporated into the Borough of Luton on 1 April 1933, Stopsley, as a village, has managed to retain its own identity. Taken in 1912, this photograph shows the old Post Office in Bury Road, later renamed St Thomas's Road. The *Brickmakers Arms*, the pub on the left, is a reminder of the brickmaking industry carried on in the fields nearby. Marsom Place, the row of cottages beyond the pub, has hardly changed since being built in 1903. The houses are named after Thomas Marsom, first Baptist minister in Luton and associate of John Bunyan.

82. This view of Castle Street and the *Red Lion Hotel* is still recognisable today although many of the buildings on the left have been demolished. There has been an inn on the site of the *Red Lion* since Henry VIII's suppression of the guilds in 1545. Local legend has it that this was the location of the Brothers' House of the Guild of the Holy Trinity. The *Red Lion* has served many different purposes besides being a hotel, for instance, as a customs and excise office and on another occasion a theatre where strolling players entertained customers in the stable yard.

83. In 1910 the Swedish Company S.K.F. decided to form a subsidiary company in Luton. A site was acquired and a small factory built in Skefco Road, a new road off the Leagrave Road. Employing a workforce of 150 men, the first British-made ball bearing was produced in April the following year. The factory expanded into a large industrial unit over a quarter of a mile long, completely engulfing the original Skefco Road. The company has moved to Sundon Park from the old site, but the buildings, which were designed by Sir. A. Brumwell-Thomas, still stand.

84. Luton Public Baths and Winter Assembly Hall stood in Waller Street, opposite the Grand Theatre and next door to the Plait Halls. The official opening started with an 'entertainment', arranged by Luton Amateur Swimming Club, which included a polo match between Luton and Watford. Built in 1913, these were not the first baths and pool to stand here, the previous facility opening in 1872. Segregation of the sexes was strictly enforced, with separate entrances for men and women. The heated water used in both pool and baths was supplied by two large Lancashire boilers housed in an annexe in Smith's Lane.

85. This early photograph shows the interior of the swimming baths just before the first filling. When full it contained 125,000 gallons of water. The changing cubicles can be seen on either side of the pool below the spectators' balcony, men on the left and women on the right. The polo goals were hoisted up to the roof when not in use. Autumn was the time for the swimming clubs to hold their galas. Many local factories had their own clubs and the competition, especially in polo matches, was very fierce. During the winter the pool was emptied, cubicles folded flat to the wall and the bath floored over. This provided a large hall for many activities including dancing, trade exhibitions, boxing matches, political meetings, civic banquets, poll counts, and choral and orchestral concerts.

86.   The official opening of Luton's new swimming pool took place on 27 July 1935 and was performed by the deputy mayor, Alderman G. Wistow-Walker, chairman of the Baths Committee. The open-air pool, 165-ft. long and 90-ft. wide, had a capacity of 448,000 gallons of continuously filtered and chlorinated water. Before the opening children queued from six o'clock in the morning to be the first in. After the ceremony there was a swimming and diving display given by 'The Highgate Divers' and an international water polo match between England and Wales.

87.   Local views with a winter motif were very popular in 1915 and this seasonal picture shows St Mary's, one of the largest parish churches in England.

88.   In the centre aisle of St Mary's Church stands the Rev. James O'Neill pulpit, presented to the church in 1882 by the parishioners who wished to commemorate their vicar's 20 years' ministry with them. Made from alabaster and marble, the pulpit is decorated with mosaic panels showing St Peter and the four evangelists. The Rev. James O'Neill was vicar of Luton for 34 years and a well-liked personality in religious and local affairs. At the start of his vicariate the parish of St Mary embraced the whole of Luton which he traversed at high speed in a four-wheeled gig, drawn by a large black horse called Bessie. This earned him the soubriquet of the galloping vicar!

89. The original church on this site was an old wooden building which had been brought from Woburn in 1873. The foundation stone of St Matthew's, the present church, was laid by the Duchess of Bedford in 1875 and the first service held in December the following year. Inexpensive by today's standards, it cost £5,500 to erect and had seating for 1,000 people. During the First World War, church parades were a regular feature of St Matthew's, being attended by troops billeted in the vicinity.

90. This photograph, taken in 1907, shows the first company of the Boys' Brigade to be formed in Luton. They are on parade with their fife and drum band in the playground of St Matthew's School. The movement was founded in 1883 by a Scottish Sunday School teacher named William Alexander Smith, who wanted to encourage a close bond between boys and the church. However, the introduction of drills using dummy rifles caused such an uproar that the company was disbanded. In 1925 there was a resurgence of enthusiasm, the Boys' Brigade was re-organised and six new companies were formed in Luton.

91. By 1910, due to weathering, it became necessary to carry out a maintenance and restoration operation to the exterior of St Matthew's. Money to pay for this work was raised during the previous year by holding whist drives, sales of work, Christmas bazaars and concerts. The photograph shows the elaborate scaffolding erected on the west end of the building and bell turret. A typical lashed timber structure, it seems no thought was given to the safety of the men on the upper levels. There are no safety handrails or toe boards and the ladders appear to be unfixed. Men would not be allowed to work in such conditions today.

92. In the era before the war, a popular activity at St Matthew's Church was the Men's Service Band, which, at Sunday afternoon concerts, regularly played to audiences of over 300 men in addition to supporting the organ at matins and evensong. Musicians will note the absence of a percussion section in the ensemble. Probably the drummers had been enrolled in the Boys' Brigade band. The photograph was taken in 1906 in the garden of the vicarage which stood next to the church in Boyle Street.

93. The town hall, George Street, in 1907. A hansom carriage stands on the rank outside and carters are collecting boxes, crates and cartons of hats for worldwide despatch from the railway yard.

94. After the Poor Law Act was passed in 1834, Luton combined with several of its hamlets and parishes to form an administrative union to look after the poor of the district. Until 1836, the workhouse was in Park Street, close to where the Brewery Tap stands today. Because of the greater number of poor people in the area covered by the 'Poor of Luton Union', a larger building was required. A site was chosen in Dunstable Road and the new workhouse shown in this photograph was erected. The building exists today as part of St Mary's Hospital.

95. Vauxhall Ironworks moved from London to Luton in 1905, where they amalgamated with a local firm and became known as Vauxhall and West Hydraulic Engineering Company Ltd. In the same year the first four-cylinder car was produced and the bonnet flutes that were to become so well known for the next 50 years adopted. In 1907 the company name was changed to Vauxhall Motors Ltd. During the Great War the demand for army staff cars, of which almost 2,000 were made, led to the need for increased floor space. This photograph, taken in 1916, also shows a rifle range in the bottom left corner, used by soldiers from local camps.

96. After the Great War, Vauxhall Motors continued their support of motor sport until 1923 when it was decided to concentrate on general car production. Two years later the company became a subsidiary of General Motors. In 1931 crash gearboxes were replaced by newly-designed synchro-mesh boxes, Vauxhall being the first to use them. The same year production of Bedford Commercial Vehicles was begun; many of them had wooden bodies and this necessitated a new sawmill and paint shop.

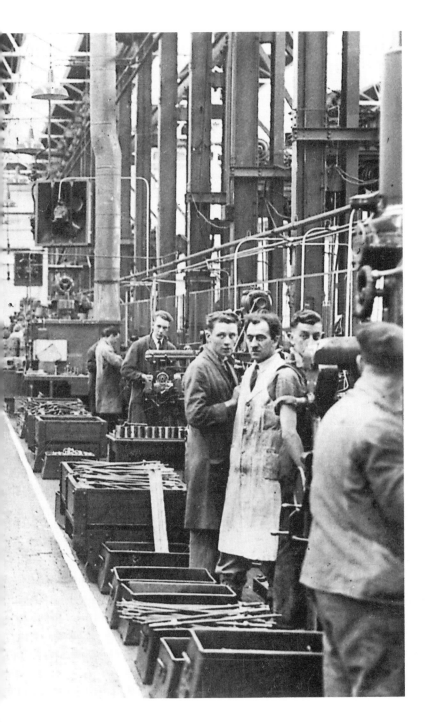

97. By the mid-1930s Vauxhall had adopted mass production. Large financial investment programmes were launched to erect new buildings, re-arrange the factory, purchase new tools and equipment to provide greater output and reduce the overall cost of the finished product. This workshop, crammed with modern machine tools producing components required for gearbox manufacture, was one of the original buildings occupied by Vauxhall Ironworks when they first came to Luton.

98. By the time Vauxhall Motors Ltd. had been established 30 years in Luton they had occupied most of the land bounded by Kimpton Road, originally called Gallows Lane, the L.M.S. main railway line, and a road called Fenny Furlong, a straggling lane that joined Park Road to Eaton Green Road. For a time Fenny Furlong actually ran through the factory as a right of way, between the car and truck body shop and the press shop. These are the two buildings on the right; the architects designed them to follow the line of the old road.

99. Being an off-shoot of General Motors, the influence of American methods of assembly were soon felt in Luton. New phrases, such as conveyor belt and working on the line or track, soon became common parlance. This photograph shows engines, destined to be installed in lorries, being assembled on a moving conveyor. The engine, starting as a cylinder block, had parts added to it by the assemblers as it slowly progressed down the 'line'. The engines were taken off as completed units and moved by an overhead conveyor to be test-run before being fitted into a waiting vehicle.

100. With the advent of mass-produced cars, panel beating and coach-built bodies became a thing of the past. Vauxhall erected a giant workshop filled with presses that could form a sheet steel roof, door or body panel in a matter of seconds. Eventually these new techniques also sounded the death knell of the car chassis, because, when welded together, the pressed body parts became sufficiently strong in themselves not to require strengthening frames.

101. To ensure that the surface of sheet steel components were blemish-free, the draw marks caused by pressing were removed by rough polishing with emery wheels. This was essential if the components were to be painted or plated. In this photograph bonnets, radiator grille surrounds and wheel arches are being cleaned prior to further surface finish treatments.

102.   Vauxhall Motors has always been proud of its recreation club. Its wide range of group activities included most hobbies; the arts, sport and social club involved thousands of employees outside working hours, encouraging a contented workforce. Probably the section that reached the largest audience was the Vauxhall Motors Orchestra, whose appearances at lunchtime concerts in the canteen, at Saturday evening dances and charity performances countrywide gave pleasure to countless listeners.

103.   It was not until the year 1220 that clerics had legal status in their diocese and as such were entitled to a vicarage provided from church monies and tithes. At this time St Mary's was Luton's only church and its vicarage was built on land between the churchyard and the River Lea. This became the traditional spot for later vicarages and most incumbents lived there, including Thomas Pomfret, father of John Pomfret the poet, after whom Pomfret Avenue was named. By the 19th century the old building had become quite imposing with a large conservatory and, in the outbuildings, its own brewhouse. This photograph shows the vicarage in the early years of the century.

104.   In the 1880s the front garden of St Mary's vicarage became known as the Adult Pleasure Garden, with an entrance from the churchyard. In 1897 Luton had a new vicar, the Rev. Edmond Mason, and high on his priority list was the selling of the old vicarage. It was bought by Luton Corporation. At this time a site was being sought for a new electricity works and it was decided to build it in the old vicarage garden. It can be seen through the trees in this postcard. The works were completed in 1901 and opened on 10 July by Lord Kelvin. Requirements for an extension six years later sealed the fate of the vicarage building and it was demolished in 1907.

105.   Until 1814 Wesleyans met in a chapel in Church Street but because of increasing congregations larger accommodation became necessary and a new chapel was built in Chapel Street. In 1834 school rooms and a new gallery were added and gas lighting installed. This enabled not only Sunday evening services to be held, but meetings and social activities during the week, a facility not available at the parish church. Attendances continued to grow and in 1851 the chapel shown in this 1910 photograph was built, providing seating for congregations of 1,800 people. The chapel was closed for worship in 1976 and in April 1979 was gutted by fire.

War and Peace, 1914~1918

106. Even before the Great War had started the War Office was anxious to encourage boys to take up a military career. These Luton boys are members of the King's Royal Rifle Corps Cadets. Their ages ranged from 12 to 16 and they were taught the skills of marching, drill and parade ground disciplines. When old enough, they qualified for immediate entry into the army without the bother of having to serve the normal basic training period. This photograph was taken at Biscot Camp in 1914.

107. Castle Street in 1915: wartime Luton, strangely devoid of traffic and almost of pedestrians, too. The *Dog Inn* on the right advertises 'Hot tea and coffee for cyclists'. This part of Castle Street invariably smelled of smouldering oak shavings, produced by T. E. Neville, the undertakers and used by Gray's the fishmonger's to cure herring and mackerel. In the distance can be seen the *Red Lion Hotel*, next door to which was an alley leading to Castle Street Hall and the smithy where Mr. Thompson the farrier had his forge.

108. As the Great War dragged on into its second year the manpower shortage became acutely noticeable and suddenly a lighter tread and knock accompanied the morning mail. Postwomen were employed on all normal postal duties except telegram deliveries. Their uniforms comprised navy serge tunics and skirts, thick overcoats with red piping and deep-crowned, broad-brimmed hats. Although they have tried to hide them with their skirts, they are also wearing lace-up boots.

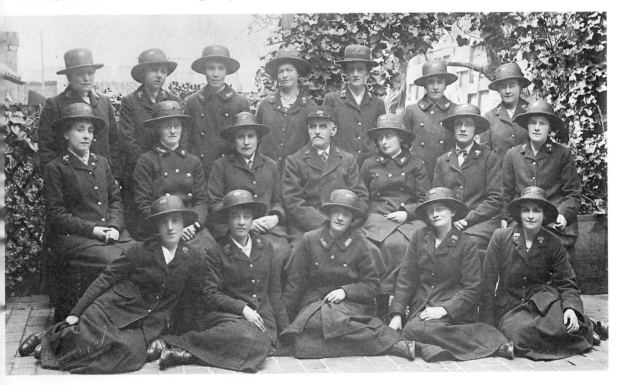

109. A balmy summer Sunday afternoon in 1915 finds Army Service Corps men from Kidney Wood Veterinary Camp relaxing with the locals around the bandstand in Wardown Park. The atmosphere is light-hearted and congenial, and the war seems a million miles away. Recognised as an easy way of finding a boyfriend, band concerts always attracted large numbers of young ladies.

110. In October 1915, bridging exercises were carried out by men of the Royal Engineers in Luton Hoo Park. Spanning the lake is the bridge they have just completed. All the joints in its construction are made with rope lashings. As a means of crossing canals and narrow rivers, pole and lashing bridges were looked on more favourably by the Royal Engineers than pontoons or boats, since the raw materials were usually to hand and did not involve the movement of bulky equipment long distances by horse-drawn transport, often under heavy gunfire.

111. Here, in New Bedford Road between Crawley Road and Mill Street, we see children enjoying the snow in the winter of 1915. One of the pictures in the 'Luton in Winter' series, it shows how severe blizzards clogged the streets in the centre of the town. Motor traffic, already reduced by petrol and spares shortages due to the war, had deserted the scene, leaving only the trams, horse-drawn vehicles and urchins to brave the elements.

112. During the great conflict, Luton was host to thousands of servicemen who were quartered in billets and camps both in and on the outskirts of the town. The soldiers could relax in the Y.M.C.A. hut when off-duty making use of the spiritual and social facilities available. On 10 April 1916 Princess Victoria Louise, eldest daughter of Queen Victoria, visited Biscot camp to open a new Y.M.C.A. hut, which was named after her.

113. The Victoria Hut had several rooms where off-duty soldiers could forget the boredom and drudgery of parade-ground and barrack-room discipline. A billiard room, canteen, padré's room, a writing room and general social room, where concerts and dances were held, gave this camp a facility for lifting morale that was envied by troops in nearby encampments.

114. This cheerful group of gunners at Biscot Camp in 1916 take time off from their fatigues and pose with this local wide boy. His make-shift stall, constructed of tea-chests and planks, displays goods to cleanse their bodies and equipment. Button sticks and polish, brushes, blanco, handkerchiefs, socks and tobacco make up the stock, but bars of lifebuoy soap seem to be the most popular line.

115. Immediately before the First World War many terraced houses were built in the new roads laid out between Ashburnham Road and Dallow Road. Intended to provide homes for the expanding workforce of the new factories opening in the Dallow Road area, they also made ideal billets for troops stationed in Luton during the conflict. Here in Lyndhurst Road in 1916 soldiers and civilians alike are mesmerised by the camera, frozen in time.

116. Newcombe Road, 1916. Photographs of street scenes like this were often produced during the war years for soldiers to send home to their loved-ones, usually marked with an 'X' to locate the sender's billet.

117. In this 1917, photograph showing the interior of the building in Church Street used by the Y.M.C.A., all appears ready for a general inspection. Everywhere is spick and span, waiting for the tide of young men who will flood through the rooms when they come off parade. The premises were provided for the soldiers stationed and billeted in Luton, in an attempt to fill the gap left by the disruption of family life due to conscription.

118. After three years of war, manpower shortages on the home front had become critical. Volunteers and conscripts to the colours had drained industry of men, so women were encouraged to take their place. This photograph of employees from the fuse shed at G. Kent Ltd., Biscot Road, clearly shows the dearth of men; there are only seven in the entire group. Note that it appeared unnecessary for the women supervisory staff to wear hair protection.

119. Although life at Biscot Camp was hard, especially during the winter months, entertainments were often organised by the troops to boost their flagging morale. This photograph, taken by an amateur photographer in 1917, shows the cast of a Pierrot Show held in the Victoria Hut. The producer of the concert party was Gunner White, seen sitting at the right-hand end of the rear row. He was a popular member of the troupe and also arranged whist drives, magic lantern shows and dances to relieve the tedium of camp life.

120.   Marching in column of fours, these First World War Tommies are returning to their billets after a day at the rifle ranges on Dallow Road hills. Strangely, one of them is dressed in civilian clothes including a flat cap and, although he is wearing a belt and ammunition pouches, he is not armed. The general store on the right has since been demolished, the resultant gap giving access to the Dallow Road Junior and Infant Schools.

121.   The men on parade here in Dallow Road Recreation Ground in 1917 are a Signal Company of the Royal Engineers. They provided a variety of services to the army, which included passing messages by means of heliographs, semaphore, pigeons and runners. The signalling flags they used can be seen strapped to their cycle cross-bars. Their support vehicles and horses are in the park behind them, and the covered wagon contains bundles of striped ranging poles, used to assess the best 'lay' for signalling points.

122.   This group of women, posing in their overalls and wearing protective gauze breathing masks, worked at the munition filling factories at Chaul End. The safety clothing was necessary to minimise the effects of the hazardous chemicals used in the contents of the shells, bombs and grenades they were producing during the First World War. The main ingredient in these weapons was phenol or picric acid which coloured the skin yellow on contact and caused the operators to become known as 'canary girls'.

123.   Chaul End Lane, 1929. Industry, commerce and improved roads have eroded this rural scene. The Cosgrove Factory Estate fills the fields where cows once grazed and Chaul End Lane has become a busy highway joining the Dunstable Road and the A505 relief road. The signal box and home of the L.N.E.R. level-crossing keeper have long since gone and the gates have fallen into disrepair. Trains stopped at Chaul End Halt, bringing the 'canary girls' to and from the shell filling factory in Connaught Road.

124.   Lady Luck has been unkind to this group of artillerymen at Biscot Camp in 1918. They did not expect the rigours of winter late into April. Bell tents are not the ideal sleeping quarters in wet, slushy conditions, but the men probably preferred the Biscot mud to that of Flanders, whether it was summer or winter.

125. A crowd gathers to watch members of the Bedford branch of the National Federation of Discharged and Demobilised Soldiers and Sailors Association march from Stuart Street into Chapel Street in 1919. The Federation was formed in 1917, and members were among those refused permission to hold a drumhead service in Wardown Park on Peace Celebration Day.

126. To celebrate Peace Day, Luton school children were to be presented with a medal, a gift from the Mayor, Henry Impey. Unfortunately the manufacturers were unable to meet the delivery date. They were not ready for distribution until mid-August, when the children were on their summer holidays! This was another of the irritations that fuelled the anti-Council feeling before the Peace Day Riots.

127. The tableau intended to epitomise the Peace Day celebrations was entitled 'Peace Enthroned', featuring a girl dressed as the Princess of Peace, holding a bouquet of white lilies. Her attendants were two children dressed in white, each clutching a lyre. The group sat under a hemispherical canopy representing the countries involved in the Great War.

128. An unexpected last minute entry for the procession caught the organisers by surprise. The tableau was called 'Jack Cornwell, V.C.', and was a mock-up of a naval gun turret mounted on a flat cart and pulled by ex-servicemen and naval ratings on leave.

129. As the Peace Day procession moves down Market Hill towards the town hall, women war-workers from Kent's ride past on the back of a decorated lorry, assembling fuses and detonators. They are followed by a company of girl guides, the Hayward-Tyler Company float and Peace Enthroned. Note the man standing on the first-floor window-sill of Blundell Brothers.

130. At lunchtime on Peace Day, crowds outside the town hall stood in a steady drizzle, while others watched from shop and office windows. Little did they realise that later in the day the windows of S. Farmer and Co. would be smashed and the grand pianos pulled out onto the pavement.

131. Driving through George Street near Cheapside is the Hayward-Tyler Co. lorry, on the back of which are pumps and aerated mineral water-making machinery as supplied to many of the navy's ships. Two employees dressed as sailors in tropical whites add a touch of realism.

132. At the corner of North Street and Old Bedford Road stands the *Rabbit*, which was built in 1908. It was here that many of the disgruntled ex-servicemen and their sympathisers spent the afternoon and evening prior to joining the disturbances in George Street during the Peace Day celebrations on 19 July 1919.

133. This cartoon well illustrates the wild night that concluded the Luton Peace Day celebrations; fire engines attacked, hoses cut, baton-wielding police, the mob drenched with water, looting, fighting and the set-piece, the old town hall ablaze from end to end.

To Commemorate "Peace" Town Hall "Goes West".

134. The scene at the drumhead memorial service held in Luton Hoo Park on 27 July 1919, one week after the Peace Day riot. Lady Wernher (with stick), Lady of the Manor of Luton and owner of Luton Hoo Park, can be seen with some of the 20,000 townsfolk who attended the ceremony, which passed off peacefully. Shortly afterwards Lady Wernher remarried and became Lady Ludlow.

135. On 10 December 1922 Lady Ludlow unveiled the war memorial, commemorating Luton's dead in the Great War. It was erected on the spot where, only three years previously, rioters had stood in front of their blazing town hall. The cost of the memorial was £4,000 and was met by public subscription. The photograph shows the crowd that packed George Street at the unveiling ceremony.

136. The Peace Day riot left the town hall in ruins and a scar in the centre of the town. With the impending unveiling of the war memorial in 1922, the site of the old town hall was obscured by a tall cedar-wood panelled fence. Note the Penfold hexagonal pillar box to the right of the centre lamp standard. This box has been preserved and is now outside the Wardown Museum and Art Gallery.

137. After the First World War, Lady Ludlow presented a new park to the people of Luton, in memory of her son Alex Pigott Wernher, who was killed in action in France during 1916. The park contained a bandstand, tennis courts, putting green, bowling green and shop. At a ceremony in 1922, a memorial to her son was unveiled and the land and gardens in West Hill/Tennyson Road officially named the Luton Hoo Memorial Park.

138. Following the burning of the old town hall the administration of Luton was carried out in offices spread throughout the town and full Council meetings were held in the Carnegie Library. By 1931 the initial designs for the replacement hall were complete but later in the year were shelved because of the national financial crisis. In 1934 the plans were approved by the Ministry of Health and the first brick laid the following year. On 30 May 1935 the foundation stone was laid and on 28 October 1936 H.R.H. The Duke of Kent opened Luton's new town hall, 17 years after the loss of the earlier building.

Transportation

139. This photograph shows the Midland railway station as it was in 1908, with few pedestrians and even fewer horse-drawn vehicles. The building was opened in the late 1860s in a curious blend of architectural styles ranging from Swiss Alpine to Victorian Chapel. Crossing Station Road at high level can be seen the spans of the lattice footbridge that connected Bute Street and Midland Road.

140. Drawn up as though on platform parade are some of the many members of staff employed at the Midland railway station in 1907. The entrance hall and ticket office were on the right-hand platform, giving entry from Station Road. Passengers travelling to London crossed the railway lines by means of the covered bridge to reach the 'up' line. The cantilevered canopies over the platforms were designed as weather protection for waiting passengers and were the epitome of embellished Victoriana.

The Race for the
Morning Train at Luton

141. A direct rail link between Luton and London began in October 1868, offering undreamed of opportunities for Lutonians. Excursions, holidays, transport of raw materials and despatch of finished products, especially hats, promised a rosy future for businessmen and general public alike. By the time this humorous card appeared in 1909, low-cost 'workmen's tickets' were on sale, the early morning workman's return to London costing less than 2 shillings!

142. When the railway lines were laid through Luton, High Town was virtually isolated from the rest of the town. To rectify this a footbridge was built spanning the tracks. The bridge, which also gave access to both stations, was officially opened on 28 April 1868. It replaced an ancient track connecting Bute Street with a narrow lane, known as Back Street in High Town.

143. Hansom cab in Williamson Street, *c*.1906. Named after carriage designer J. A. Hansom, these two-wheeled vehicles had the driver's seat outside at the rear; the passengers sitting inside were protected from the elements by two small doors which, when closed, gave privacy, too. At slack times cabs parked outside public buildings in recognised spaces called cab ranks. In Luton there were ranks outside the town hall, the railway stations and the free library in Williamson Street. The hansom cabs were licensed to ply for hire by the Council; strict rules and inspection ensured the driver, or cabbie, fed the horse and kept it in good condition.

144. Before the advent of motorised public transport travellers had to rely on horse-drawn buses. The route of this bus started at Manchester Square, Luton, and terminated at the *Sugar Loaf*, Leagrave. Suspension was by leaf springs on both axles, while steering was effected by the horses moving a single shaft coupled to the front axle. When required, the driver could operate a linkage to open louvred windows in the saloon to extract stale air and tobacco smoke.

145. In 1906 both hansom cabs and horse-drawn buses were in service on Luton streets, in this case New Bedford Road. A favourite stretch of road for courting couples, it was known as 'the bunny run' or 'the monkey parade'. The buses were called 'garden seat buses', because of the spartan slatted wooden seats. On the other hand, the cabs provided a luxurious interior and ride for the monied or romantic client.

146a. & b. The brakes, one shown on a local letter heading and the other about to transport the customers of the *Engine* in Bute Street, were essentially short-haul waggons, suitable for local journeys or visiting beauty spots like Barton, Gustard Wood, Ashridge and the Downs. Routes had to be carefully planned to avoid steep hills, or tired and stubborn horses could mar an otherwise happy outing.

147.   An interior view of the Luton Tramways Depot in Park Street. Taken in February 1908, it shows the newly assembled trams prior to the official opening. Some idea of the size of the building can be gained from the three trams parked end to end on the left.

148.   This group photograph shows the crews, inspectors, maintenance staff and management of the Luton Corporation Tramways in the Park Street Depot at the official opening in February 1908. Notice the wheelwright in shirtsleeves on the left. One of his jobs was to shrink new steel tyres on worn iron bogie wheels.

149.   Tram breakdown in New Bedford Road, *c.*1908. A policeman always attended such incidents, in case passengers became too irate.

150.   In 1910, when this photograph was taken, the hamlet of Round Green stood mid-way between Luton and Stopsley. The tracks bringing the trams from George Street and up through High Town ended here outside the *Jolly Topers*. After the passengers had alighted the driver would disconnect the current collector pole from the overhead electricity supply cable and turn it about for the return journey.

151. Old No.13 was a single-decker tram and a familiar sight on the Wardown route. It was a converted horse-drawn tram which had previously seen service in Glasgow. This tram was operated by one man who drove it as well as collecting the fares and issuing tickets.

152. By 1914 trams were an accepted part of Luton's street scene and their popularity was endorsed by Council Tramway Committee reports claiming between two and three million passengers carried per year. This photograph highlights the difficult nature of the routes they travelled. The steep hills on either side of the Lea Valley caused motor wear when climbing and braking troubles when descending. Tight turns around existing street corners caused excessive wear on the tram's steel-tyred wheels.

153. The Christ Church Women's Club sitting in a Palladian charabanc parked in Inkerman Street, awaiting the start of their annual outing in 1921. The vehicle was bought in 1920 as a lorry and subsequently fitted with the charabanc body. It belonged to Bluebird Motors and was garaged in Bedford Road. The drivers called it 'the two choice chara' because passengers could sit either in the fixed roof saloon at the rear, or in the open air at the front.

154. When first purchased, the upper deck of trams was open to the sky, which, although pleasant in the summer, proved quite unacceptable in the wind and rain of winter. In the late 1920s privately-owned saloon-bodied buses appeared in the streets, so in 1930 the Council made an attempt to lure back lost passengers by fitting four cars with roofs. The conversions cost £250 per tram, but did little to help the ailing service. The photograph shows both open-topped and roofed trams side by side in George Street in 1930.

155. After the trams were withdrawn from service in 1932, the Corporation replaced them with maroon and cream
coloured buses which plied the same routes. The buses were also garaged in the old tram depot in Park Street. One of the
new buses can be seen passing the Alma, a picture palace built towards the end of the tram era. The *Luton News* office is
on the left and the *Crown and Anchor* can be seen on the right.

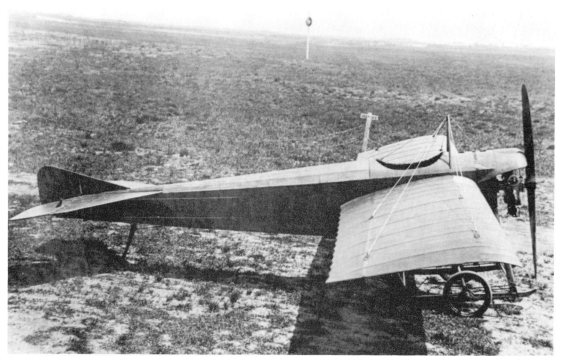

156. The company of Hewlett and Blondeau had seen the commercial possibilities of aircraft manufacture several years before the Great War and built several planes to other people's designs. This single seat, rotary-engined Dyott Monoplane is seen at their airstrip at Oakley Road, the present site of the Electrolux Factory, shortly after Bleriot flew the English Channel in 1909.

157. Hewlett and Blondeau produced several types of aircraft for the Royal Flying Corps and later the Royal Air Force, including the famous Avro 504-K. They had a varying degree of success with other aircraft. The Dyott twin-engined bomber, for instance, was a failure, whilst the single-engined, two-seater biplane shown here, code named BE-2-C, was used quite successfully on light bombing and reconnaissance missions on the Western Front between 1915 and 1917. During this time the factory turned out 15 aeroplanes a week.

158. In the late 1920s and early 1930s the visit of a flying circus always caused a stir of excitement. Crowds flocked to Lewsey Farm to see Alan Cobham, later Sir Alan, and his fliers put their machines through their paces. Acrobatics, walking on the wings and parachute drops held the crowd spellbound and after the display people queued for hours to experience the thrill of a half-a-crown flip.

Parades, Processions and Events

159. In 1899 the first prize for a decorated cart in the Luton charity fête procession was won by the Luton Amateur Swimming Club's entry called The Wild Duck Houseboat. It represented the sort of floating shooting lodges used by the aristocracy for parties and duck shoots held on rivers and broads. After the judging and prize-giving, this float was presented to the children's home in London Road, re-erected in the grounds, and used by the patients and staff as a summer house.

160. By 1907 the desire to win first prize in the charity procession was so strong that thousands of man-hours went into the design and preparation of floats. This spectacular entry in the lifeboat fête procession of that year represented a palace in paradise and, although peopled by a dozen well-dressed Lutonians, was only pulled by one horse. It was decorated with exotic plants and foliage, set off by the trellis fencing. The secretary of the National Lifeboat Institution described it as 'the finest float ever built in the country to take part in a lifeboat procession'.

161. Parades have always been popular events in Luton, especially among milliners, for as you can see there is scarcely a bare head. This was the United Red Cross church parade of 1910, marching along New Bedford Road. Charity parades usually mustered in Wardown Park, marched through the town to St Mary's Church and were followed by a civic service.

162 & 163. Political occasions always roused strong feelings of passion in the town as can be seen by the large number of Lutonians gathered outside the town hall to hear the result of the general election in 1906. The returning officer is introducing the successful Liberal member of parliament for Luton, Mr. Thomas Gair Ashton, a businessman from Cheshire. He had been re-elected, for this was not the first time he represented the Luton Division. In 1895 he was elected for South Bedfordshire, Luton Division, and successfully defended the seat in the next four elections. He was Luton's member for 16 years and in 1910 was created Lord Ashton of Hyde.

164. The Luton Amateur Operatic and Dramatic Society take their bow following a performance of 'The Pirates of Penzance' at the Grand Theatre in 1907.

165. Playing bowls in Luton did not become possible until Wardown Park was acquired and a public green established there in 1905. The game caught on very quickly and greens were soon laid in other parks, clubs and factory sports fields until by 1930 there were at least 12 clubs in the town. This photograph was taken in about 1908 in Wardown Park.

166.   The audience at the opening of the Premier Skating Rink in about 1906: all appear to be wearing their Sunday best and do not look in the least like skaters. The Premier Rink stood just off Park Street, near Cumberland's Yard, and when skating lost its appeal, the building was turned into a billiard hall.

167. The Bone family, who owned a musical instrument shop in New Bedford Road, were committed to encouraging the enjoyment of music in Luton. Mr. Philip Bone was a tutor for most stringed instruments and in 1896 founded a Mandolin Band which bore his name. About 10 years later the band became nationally famous and its name changed to the Luton Mandolin Band.

MACHINING HAT.

BLOCKING HAT.

FROM LUTON

MAKING THE LARGEST STRAW HAT IN THE WORLD

168. The gentlemen holding this outsize boater in 1910 are claiming it as the largest in the world. It measured 7ft. 6in. across the brim and the crown was 2ft. high. Exhibition hats similar to this were made of 'jumbo' plait an inch wide, of which 200 yards were needed to complete them. Notice that the hat was so large that when pressing the crown it was necessary for the blocker to stand on the brim.

169. The Luton Borough Police Force was formed in 1876, at the time the town received its Charter of Municipal Incorporation. Initially it consisted of a chief constable, an inspector, two sergeants and eight constables. Compare this small force with the one shown in the photograph, taken in 1910. Plain-clothes officers can be seen as well as uniformed men.

170. Wedding group in Ashton Street, 1910, with the entire family in new clothes and the latest hairstyles. The boy in the bottom left-hand corner is the author's father.

171. Wardown Park was officially opened to the public on 8 July 1905. One of its most popular features was the lake, filled by diverting the River Lea. A few years later it was enlarged and decorated with an eye-catching suspension bridge and a deepwater swimming area, complete with changing pavilion. The photograph shows crowds awaiting the start of a swimming gala in 1914.

172. Luton has seen many skating rinks come and go, the first in the town being the Alexandra, which was built on a plot behind the town hall in 1880. Skating lost its popularity temporarily but regained it in 1904, when several new rinks were established, among them Park Street, Leagrave Road, Ramridge Road, and the American Roller Skating Rink in Dunstable Road opposite the gas works offices, shown here *c.*1912.

173. This was the scene at the first Luton Motor Club Rally to be held after the First World War. The scars of the Peace Day riot are beginning to disappear, with the remains of the old town hall hidden behind the fence. The club met in George Street and, although described as a car rally, only motor cycles have turned up. What strange devices they are, with girder forks, hand change gearboxes, belt drive, 'square' petrol tanks and rubber bulb horns.

174. On 17 November 1926 the Luton fire brigade formed a triumphal arch with fire escapes outside the St Mary's Road fire station to greet the Prince of Wales. The object of his visit was to present new colours and drums to the 2nd Battalion, Beds. and Herts. Regiment. To the left of the fire station is St Mary's School and Hall, while in the background is the chimney of the Luton Electricity Works.

Family Businesses

S. Farmer & Co's Pianos.

The New 'Boudoir' Model,

23 GUINEAS CASH, or 14/6 per month easy terms.

Has a sustaining musical quality of tone, combined with
solidity of construction, and perfect finish and design.

Incomparable
Value.

S. Farmer and Co. wish it to be clearly understood that the UTMOST VALUE
and attention is given to the interior construction and workmanship,
no money being wasted in unnecessarily elaborate cases.

Sole Agents: S. FARMER & Co., Piano Merchants,

2, Wellington Street and 85, George Street,

Branch: 3, West Street, Dunstable.

LUTON.

A Dunstable customer writes:

"I cannot refrain from writing to say how pleased I am with the Piano you supplied a year or more ago. It has given every satisfaction, and the tone improves with age."

A Hitchin gentleman writes:

"I am simply charmed with the Piano, more I cannot say. With my best thanks for your advice and kindness."

175. The showrooms of S. Farmer and Co. were always well stocked with the best
selection of pianos and organs in the district. They were particularly proud to be
able to claim 'Brinsmead's Pianos, By Appointment to H.R.H. The Prince of
Wales'. In 1907 'boudoir' pianos were all the rage, intended for a woman's private
bedroom. It was from the broken windows of this shop that pianos were pulled onto
the pavement to entertain the rioters the night the town hall was burned down in
1919. A photograph of the shop frontage is shown in plate 130.

176. In 1840 two Luton men named Brown and Green founded a general and furnishing ironmonger's business on Market Hill. Two years later, due to increased trade, they moved to new premises in George Street, a site their business was to occupy until 1963. In 1844, wishing to diversify their activities, Brown and Green started Luton's first iron foundry and disposed of the ironmongery part of the firm to Mr. G. F. Gibbs. After 50 years in the trade, Mr. Gibbs sold the company to two brothers named Dandy, newly arrived in the town from Peterborough. They realised that Gibbs' name would ensure continuity of trade and so called their newly acquired business Gibbs and Dandy. In 1990 the company celebrates its 150th anniversary.

177. Duberly and White, Chemists, were established in 1825, starting with a small shop next to the entrance of Pearman's brewery on Market Hill. However, tending the needs of 'delicate children and consumptives' must have paid off, for they soon opened another shop in Park Street and by the early 1930s had premises in Dunstable Road and New Bedford Road, too.

178. This 1907 advertisement recalls the days when every railway station and halt had its own coalyard. The railways, coalburners themselves, made an ideal distribution network for the fuel. It also shows that rising prices began well before the 1980s and '90s.

MOTTO - "KEEP MOVING."

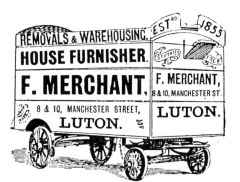

ESTIMATES

FREE.

ESTIMATES

FREE.

F. Merchant & Sons,

COMPLETE HOUSE FURNISHERS,

8 & 10,

Manchester Street, Luton.

CABINET MAKERS.

Upholsterers and French Polishers.

MAKERS OF INSIDE AND OUTSIDE BLINDS.

THE LUTON ELECTRIC CARPET BEATING WORKS

179. F. Merchant and Sons was a family business established in 1855, supplying household furnishings and carpets. Their salerooms, as opposed to showrooms, were in Manchester Street. Delivery could be made from stock on the day of purchase. This advertisement appeared in 1907.

180. Before the era of public transport, when much travel was done on foot, most towns had many shoe shops, generally stocked with Northampton-made products. Before the Great War, there were over 150 businesses involved in the shoe trade in Luton. However, affluent purchasers could buy shoes made on their own personal lasts from bespoke bootmakers. Skelton and Son had workshops at the rear of their premises in Wellington Street for making and storing customers' lasts. They also made leather and cloth leggings and gaiters, cut to the customer's own style.

181. The ironmonger's shop at 44/46, Chapel Street spanned almost 75 years, having been opened by Mr. C. W. Ward just before the turn of the century and closed under the ownership of G. and A. Bryant Ltd. in the early 1970s. Mr. Tydeman, who owned the business for some 40 years, was well known in the town for selling snowflake crystal oil, a refined paraffin used as a fuel for oil lamps which, it was claimed, 'gave no smoke, no smell and shed a pure white light', and all for 10d. per gallon.

182. Waller's grocery shop stood in Cumberland Street, named after John Cumberland who established Luton's off-street cattle markets. The site of the shop now lies under the foundations of Dunham and Haines car showrooms. Although Waller's stopped trading in the early 1930s, it was typical of almost 200 grocery shops to be found in Luton before the emergence of the supermarkets in the 1950s, and provided a local service to the terraced houses of Park Town, a district away from the town centre.

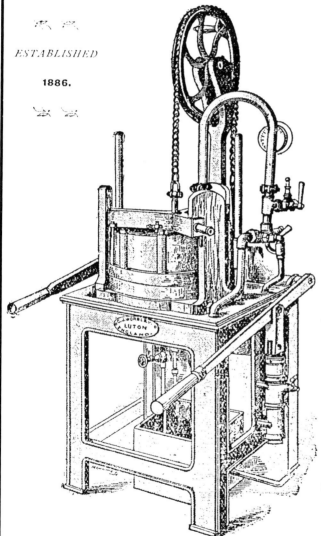